THE WORLD OF THE
FOUR FREEDOMS

THE WORLD OF THE
FOUR FREEDOMS

By SUMNER WELLES

With a Foreword by

NICHOLAS MURRAY BUTLER

COLUMBIA UNIVERSITY PRESS

New York · Morningside Heights · 1943

Foreword

THIS volume of addresses, delivered during the past three years by the distinguished Under Secretary of State, the Honorable Sumner Welles, may well become a classic. These pages contain in simple, direct, and convincing form a unique presentation of the present world situation, particularly as it affects the Government and the people of the United States. Here are recorded and clearly presented the facts which led to the collapse of Woodrow Wilson's great effort to end international war by a farsighted and public-spirited plan for international cooperation. Here are recorded the outstanding facts relating to the present colossal world-wide struggle for gain and for power on the part of the aggressor nations in Europe and in Asia. Here are presented the considerations which should guide the thought and the policy of the whole world, and particularly those of the American people, when this war shall have come to an end. At that time, the people of the United States must be prepared to say most emphatically: This shall not happen again.

The reader of these pages will find—perhaps for the first time—a record of the acts and words of that group of leaders in American political life who dashed the hopes of the United States and of the world by preventing the constructive policies associated with the name of Woodrow Wilson from being put into practical effect. These were in the interest and defense of every American. It may well be that the future historian will point to these political leaders and their acts as a chief cause in making possible the world war which rages today.

[v]

Not many Americans remember the fact that in June, 1910, nearly thirty-three years ago, the Congress of the United States by the unanimous vote of both Houses called upon the President to invite the nations of the world to organize for the establishment of international peace, this organization to be protected by an international police force made up of the combined navies of the world. When this vote was taken there was not a single dissent—Republican or Democrat—in the Senate or the House of Representatives. Therefore, when a few years later Woodrow Wilson proposed his plan for an organized society of nations, he was simply acting under what may properly be called the instructions of the Congress of the United States. That there was no difference between the political parties on this great issue is made plain by the fact that when Warren G. Harding was conducting his campaign for the Presidency in 1920, he used these words in a noteworthy speech delivered in the State of Ohio:

The other type is a society of free nations, or an association of free nations, or a league of free nations, animated by considerations of right and justice, instead of might and self-interest, and not merely proclaimed an agency in pursuit of peace, but so organized and so participated in as to make the actual attainment of peace a reasonable possibility. Such an association I favor with all my heart, and I would make no fine distinction as to whom credit is due. One need not care what it is called. Let it be an association, a society, or a league, or what not, our concern is solely with the substance, not the form thereof.

Moreover, the platforms of both great American political parties endorsed participation and leadership in the movement for world organization to secure prosperity and peace upon foundations of justice and moral political philosophy.

Under Secretary Welles makes it plain in these pages what has been the result of the fact that these solemn pledges to the people were not kept by their elected representatives.

When President McKinley more than forty years ago used his famous sentence—"The period of exclusiveness is past"—he pointed the path of progress upon which American political policy should enter and made the doctrine of national isolation ridiculous.

Under Secretary Welles discusses all these and related matters in the light of today. His book should be read and reflected upon by every intelligent American.

It should be added that these addresses are published at the urgent invitation of Columbia University, which records its appreciation of the generous action of the author in granting to the University the necessary permission.

NICHOLAS MURRAY BUTLER

Columbia University
March 1, 1943

Contents

CONTENTS

On the Margin
of War

IN ACCORDANCE with the principles of the
Convention for the Maintenance, Preservation, and
Reestablishment of Peace, the Declaration of Inter-
American Solidarity of Buenos Aires, and the Declaration of Lima, the Ministers of Foreign Relations of the
American Republics or their representatives are meeting here in Panama for the purpose of consultation. Under the terms of the agreements I have cited, this coming
together to consult is not an undertaking into which we
have entered lightly. We have, on the contrary, agreed
and clearly stipulated that the consultation provided
for in these agreements shall be undertaken when there
exists in the belief of our respective governments a menace to the peace of the continent.

I speak, of course, solely in the name of my own Government, but I venture to assert that the government of
every American Republic coincides in the opinion that
the outbreak of the general war with which the world
today is confronted constitutes in very truth a potential
menace to the well-being, to the security, and to the
peace of the New World. And it is for that reason that
we are meeting here in this historic city of Panama. We

are today creating a precedent. The Conference for the Maintenance of Peace of Buenos Aires was called, as we all recognize, for the specific purpose of reaching a common understanding while world peace existed as to how the nations of the New World might best safeguard their legitimate interests and most readily preserve the peace of their own peoples in the event that war broke out in other parts of the world.

The meeting here assembled is the first and the direct result of the engagements undertaken at the Conference of Buenos Aires. It is a meeting of the American neighbors to consider, in a moment of grave emergency, the peaceful measures which they may feel it wise to adopt either individually or jointly, so as best to insure their national interests and the collective interests of the nations of the New World.

And it is singularly fitting that this great practical demonstration of inter-American solidarity should be realized in Panama. Every one of us who meets here today will recognize that this assembly constitutes the realization of an ideal—the realization of the vision that Bolivar possessed more than a century ago—an ideal which time and again it had seemed could never be attained. It lies within the power of those of us who have the privilege of representing our governments upon this occasion to insure not only the attainment of that ideal, but also by so doing to insure the lasting establishment of a peaceful form of practical cooperation and interdependence between equal and sovereign states on a scale which the world has rarely witnessed and which, at this moment, is more than ever imperative.

The purpose for which we meet and the topics which

will come up for consideration are clearly set forth in the agenda upon which we have agreed. As my Government envisages it, it is our common desire to take under consideration the complicated question of our rights and duties as neutrals, in view of the outbreak of general war in Europe, with a view to the preservation of the peace of our respective nations and with a view towards obtaining complete respect on the part of all belligerents for our respective sovereignties. It would seem to me desirable, so far as conditions and our untrammeled rights of individual action make it possible, for us in this connection to give some thought to the desirability of our reaching some uniform standards of approach with regard to the steps which we may individually take in determining and in asserting our rights and obligations as neutrals. It would seem to me to be self-evident that should it be possible to attain such an objective, our individual capacity to maintain our sovereign rights unimpaired, as well as our ability to preserve the peace of our continent, would be correspondingly enhanced.

We are further agreed that we will give the fullest consideration to all measures which we may individually or collectively undertake to preserve the American continent free from conflict and to keep war away from our New World.

Finally, we are agreed that we will undertake to discuss and to consider those practical steps which can most advantageously be undertaken to cushion our national economies from the shock of the war which has broken out and to prevent so far as may be possible that disruption and dislocation of inter-American economic, financial, and commercial intercourse which wrought such havoc during the years of the Great War of 1914–18. We are also in accord that we will give thought to the continuation and expansion of long-range programs for commercial and economic cooperation among our several Republics.

In the economic sphere the struggle that is going on confronts us with difficulties of both an immediate and an ultimate character. We are already experiencing dislocations in our usual commerce. Some of the markets for our products will be closed or diminished; others will be greatly changed. We must anticipate difficulties in disposing of war-created surpluses in some directions which will result in lowering prices or in bringing new burdens to our public finances. In other directions we must anticipate an abnormally increased demand which will result in price increases, unexpected gains, and the dangers of expansion on temporary and unstable foundations.

Each of our nations will no doubt determine upon a program aimed to lessen the effects upon its own welfare of these dislocations. But there are many ways in which the American Republics can assist each other in the task. We may be able, without undertaking discriminations against the rest of the world, substantially to increase our commerce with one another. Countries which have similar surplus problems may be able to devise temporary arrangements with each other that will ameliorate their situation. By our concerted effort we may be able to achieve something in the maintenance of our usual trade in staple peacetime commodities with other neutral countries.

We all of us remember only too well the havoc which

was occasioned our inter-American economic system
after the war broke out in 1914. Inter-American shipping communications were either abandoned or were
seriously crippled; the legitimate export trade of many
Republics—even that to their American neighbors, upon
which in great part their national economy depended—
was disrupted or destroyed with resultant misery and
distress to their respective peoples. It appears to my
Government that the opportunity is now afforded for
us severally to assure ourselves and each other that this
will not occur again.

So far as my own Government is concerned, I am authorized to state that so long as the present situation
continues, the regular transportation facilities of the
shipping lines between the United States and its American neighbors now in operation will not only not be
curtailed, but will be strengthened and increased, whenever such increase may be found to be desirable and
feasible.

Financial assistance and cooperation may be developed to tide over short emergency periods and to
develop in individual countries new fields of production
to replace those temporarily depressed.

I am authorized to state that the United States Government wishes to cooperate with all other American
Republics in such efforts of each to develop the resources
of its country along sound economic and noncompetitive
lines. When desired it will assist in making credit available to them through the services and facilities of its
privately-owned banking system as well as its Govern-
ment-owned agencies when the latter have funds available for such purposes.

In financing current matters, it is expected that only short-term credits will be requested, but in the purchase of rail and mill equipment, heavy goods, et cetera, longer term credits appropriate to the circumstances will be required. Also it is of course recognized that war conditions may shift certain international trade markets, and this will need to be taken into account.

My Government likewise recognizes that excessive or unwarranted fluctuations in inter-American exchanges brought about by conditions resulting from the war situation would seriously prejudice beneficial trade between the American Republics. It is my hope that our deliberations may result in agreement. To the extent that we sustain bases of commercial policy that are universal in character and leave trade open to all countries on substantially the same terms, and to the extent that our commerce is not dictated by special agreements of an exclusive character, to that extent can we insure that our political independence cannot be subjugated to alien political systems operating through commercial channels.

There is also incumbent upon us the task of keeping vigorous our belief that work and production should be primarily for peaceful welfare. If by our joint effort and strength we keep this continent free from the threat of aggression, we will greatly lessen the need of subordinating our individual productive energies by making preparatory arrangements which may assist in safeguarding against this danger.

These, as I understand them, are the specific and practical measures which we are called upon to consider. They are all of them problems of vital importance to the

American Republics—problems of the highest and most legitimate self-interest; but we all of us recognize, I am sure, that however much we may desire to insulate ourselves from the effects of this present conflict, such insulation can be only relative. It cannot in any event do more than mitigate in so far as we are able the disasters which will affect all peoples, belligerent or neutral, as a result of this world calamity.

Beyond these immediate problems produced by the war crisis there are problems which are deeper and more fundamental. We have prospered by regarding our commerce and production as designed to serve, through the exercise of individual initiative, the ends of public welfare and not the ends of political strategy. We shall be faced by the fact that various powerful countries in other parts of the world have now completely converted their own system of trade and production to another basis— making it an instrument of political or ideological ambition. By common determination and cooperation we can do much to avoid having our own purposes dominated by those of others or subordinated to military demands. But, since in these days it is essential to be strong (for we have seen all too often the fate of the weak), we can make every effort to see that our program of defense is of a character that reaffirms our faith in the powers of individual initiative and of free men. We can draw our strength from our liberties and from the contribution of men and women become strong and disciplined under conditions of freedom.

I believe that the time has come when the twenty-one American Republics must state, and state clearly and in no uncertain terms, to all of the belligerents, both as a right of self-protection and as a right inherent in their position as peaceful and independent powers, constituting an entire continent remote from the causes of the hostilities which have broken out, that they cannot agree that their security, their nationals, or their legitimate commercial rights and interests should be jeopardized by belligerent activities in close proximity to the shores of the New World. This assertion of principle, I believe, must be regarded as constituting a declaration of the inalienable right of the American Republics to protect themselves, so far as conditions in this modern world make it possible, from the dangers and the repercussions of a war which has broken out thousands of miles from their shores and in which they are not involved.

But in the larger sense, every one of our nations, every one of our fellow citizens, is affected or will be affected by the growing tragedy of this new war.

War spells ruin, waste, torture, and death—not, perhaps, to the leaders who have wrought it, but to the countless numbers of humble men and women throughout the world who would have none of it. For there is nothing surer in the world today than that the vast mass of the common people everywhere have wanted above all else to prevent the war which has now broken out.

Far removed from the initial scene of hostilities as the peoples of the Americas are, their interests have been jeopardized by the commencement of war. In modern civilization, every country has a natural right that war shall not be loosed upon humanity. This right was subscribed to by every nation of the civilized world in the so-called Pact of Paris, and it is this right, so solemnly subscribed to, that is today being flagrantly violated.

[8]

There is no moral justification for any nation to loose war upon humanity when the resort to peaceful procedure for the solution of controversies or of inequities is available.

The only possible road for achieving peace is through cooperation; this implies the juridic equality of every nation and the acceptance of a moral order and of effective international law. It assumes that controversies will be settled by peaceful processes and that all peoples will under these pacific processes cooperate on equal terms with generosity and with justice. It assumes that economic arrangements can be made which are entirely susceptible of satisfying the reasonable needs of any nation for beneficial trade, which will provide access on equal terms to world markets, access on equal terms to raw materials, and which will satisfy the legitimate demand of all nations for those component factors which make for a peaceful life.

There is existing now at this moment an overwhelming will on the part of peoples everywhere for peace based on renunciation of force, on justice, and on equality, could it find expression.

It may well be that the facilitation of that means of expression will be determined by the part we play in this Western Hemisphere. We, the American Republics, share in common a great heritage—the principles of democratic constitutional government, devotion to justice, respect for the pledged word, love of peace. We have created an American system, an American way of life, which is our chief contribution to world civilization. This way of life we must make every effort to protect, to safeguard, to pass on intact to future generations of our own peoples, and to maintain as an unflinching standard in a world in which each day that passes sees more standards, once believed inviolate, shattered and destroyed.

As the shadows created by the outbreak of this monstrous war darken and spread rapidly across the length and breadth of the world in which we live, the twenty-one free nations of the New World can still preserve for posterity those ideals and those beliefs which may well constitute the last great hope of the civilization which we have inherited.

Our influence for peace and for the reestablishment of a world order based on morality and on law must be unshaken and secure. To accomplish this we must, and we can, resolutely defend our continent from all menace of aggression, direct or indirect. To do so, we must make every effort to keep alive our liberal commercial policy in our relations with those other nations of the world who are willing to join with us. To do so, we must strengthen and fortify the solidarity of understanding and the identity of individual purpose which bind us closely together. To do so, we must rely ever more resolutely upon the principles of freedom and of democracy and upon the ideals of our Christian faith, through which our nations have had their being and only through which can their future rest secure.

An Association
of Nations

WE ARE MET here today to join in the dedication of the new wing of the Norwegian Legation in Washington. These ceremonies are surely symbolic of the hope and of the faith with which we meet. Those of us who are citizens of the United States are taking part in these dedication ceremonies not only because of the welcome privilege which it affords us of rendering this tribute to our traditional friends, the heroic people of Norway, but also because we can thus best evidence our conviction that the Kingdom of Norway of the past, as we have known it, some day—and we trust that day will come soon—will once more be free and independent.

We here in the United States will always remember the superb courage with which the Norwegian people fought in the defense of their homes and of their liberties against the overwhelmingly superior strength of an invader who had treacherously taken them by surprise. We know how bravely they are still fighting with their allies on sea and land in many parts of the world.

We shall always remember the heroism of their Monarch and of their Crown Prince. And we have heard with emotion the words of that same Monarch when he said to his people only a few days ago, "Hold out. Don't lose courage. And be assured that Norway will once again be free and independent, provided that we all continue to do our duty and our utmost to reach our goal in the battle which is now being fought."

Those words seem to us to exemplify the soul of a people which will never admit defeat and which will never be cowed by alien domination.

But in a larger sense, these ceremonies constitute an act of faith in the ultimate victory of the forces of human liberty, in the triumph of civilization itself over the forces of barbarism.

I feel that there are joined with us in spirit here today, as silent witnesses, the peoples of all of the other countries which have been mercilessly overrun during these past two years. I know that they believe as we do that out of this holocaust into which the nations of the earth have been plunged by the criminal obsession of world conquest of one man and of the satellites who surround him, there can come no peace until the Hitlerite government of Germany has been finally and utterly destroyed.

For I am confident that the cause of liberty and of freedom will not go down to defeat. The determination and courage of free men and women everywhere must now be exercised to the full limit of endurance until their victory is won.

And yet, I do not doubt that millions are asking to-night—millions in England and in China; millions of enslaved peoples in Norway and in the other countries now temporarily occupied; millions in the countries which have not experienced war; yes, and millions in Germany and in Italy—are asking, what does the future hold for us after this struggle is over?

Does the end of the present carnage mean only a return to ruined homes, to the graves of slaughtered wives and children, to poverty and want, to social upheaval and economic chaos, to the same gray and empty years of confusion and bitterness, so barren in vision and in human accomplishment, which marked the decades after the termination of the last war?

It seems to me that those of us who are fortunate enough to be able to live as citizens of the free American Republics have our great responsibility in the framing of the answer to that question. For we all of us now see clearly, if we did not before, that no matter how great our American capacity for defense may be, no matter how perfect our hemispheric system may become, our future welfare must inevitably be contingent upon the existence in the rest of the world of equally peace-minded and equally secure peoples who not only will not, but cannot, become a source of potential danger to us in the New World.

I feel it is not premature for me to suggest that the free governments of peace-loving nations everywhere should even now be considering and discussing the way in which they can best prepare for the better day which must come, when the present contest is ended in the victory of the forces of liberty and of human freedom and in the crushing defeat of those who are sacrificing mankind to their own lust for power and for loot.

At the end of the last war, a great President of the United States gave his life in the struggle to further the realization of the splendid vision which he had held up to the eyes of suffering humanity—the vision of an ordered world governed by law.

The League of Nations, as he conceived it, failed in part because of the blind selfishness of men here in the United States, as well as in other parts of the world; it failed because of its utilization by certain powers primarily to advance their own political and commercial ambitions; but it failed chiefly because of the fact that it was forced to operate, by those who dominated its councils, as a means of maintaining the *status quo*. It was never enabled to operate as its chief spokesman had intended, as an elastic and impartial instrument in bringing about peaceful and equitable adjustments between nations as time and circumstance proved necessary.

Some adequate instrumentality must unquestionably be found to achieve such adjustments when the nations of the earth again undertake the task of restoring law and order to a disastrously shaken world. But whatever the mechanism which may be devised, of two things I am unalterably convinced:

First, that the abolition of offensive armaments and the limitation and reduction of defensive armaments and of the tools which make the construction of such armaments possible can only be undertaken through some rigid form of international supervision and control, and that without such practical and essential control, no real disarmament can ever be achieved; and

Second, that no peace which may be made in the future would be valid or lasting unless it established fully and adequately the natural rights of all peoples to equal economic enjoyment. So long as any one people or any one government possesses a monopoly over natural resources or raw materials which are needed by all peoples, there can be no basis for a world order based on justice and on peace.

I cannot believe that peoples of good will will not once more strive to realize the great ideal of an association of nations through which the freedom, the happiness, and the security of all peoples may be achieved.

That word, security, represents the end upon which the hearts of men and women everywhere today are set. Whether it be security from bombing from the air, or from mass destruction; whether it be security from want, disease, and starvation; whether it be security in enjoying that inalienable right which every human being should possess of living out his life in peace and happiness, people throughout the length and breadth of the world are demanding security, and freedom from fear.

That is the objective before us all today—to try and find the means of bringing that to pass.

"Not in vain the distance beacons."

Commercial Policy
after the War

I DEEPLY appreciate the opportunity tonight of being the guest of the National Foreign Trade Council and of being permitted in this personal way to express my ever-increasing recognition of the public-spirited and invaluable service which has been rendered the people of the United States by the Council during these past years. I know of no comparable organization which has made a more outstanding contribution. It has throughout its existence, as was right and fitting, jealously maintained its character of complete independence as a private body, but it has, nevertheless, never failed to cooperate along helpful and complementary lines with the Government in those fields of endeavor in which the Council was primarily interested.

I think I can say with full assurance that, in the increasing gravity of the situation in which our country finds itself, the Government will have to depend ever more fully upon the constructive assistance which the Council can so ably render.

Those in attendance at this Twenty-eighth National Foreign Trade Convention are directly interested in foreign trade. But every citizen of the United States, while

[16]

perhaps individually only indirectly concerned, is nevertheless vitally affected by our foreign commerce. The prosperity of our country, the level of employment, the best interests of labor and of the consumer, and the living standards of our people depend to a very great extent upon the condition of our foreign trade.

We are all of us concerned even more deeply because the creation of conditions favorable to peaceful and profitable trade between nations is one of the cornerstones of the enduring peace which we so earnestly hope may be constructed in the place of the social wreckage and economic ruin which will inevitably result from the present war.

A very brilliant English statesman who died prematurely a few years ago once said, "It is to be specially noticed that there have nevertheless almost always existed men who sincerely, but very foolishly believed, firstly, that no war would arise in their own day, and, secondly (when that war did arise), that for some reason or other it would be the last. At this point the idealist degenerates into the pacifist; and it is at this point consequently that he becomes a danger to the community of which he is a citizen."

I cannot resign myself to that admission of human incapacity—I cannot concede the inability of man to shape his destiny, under divine guidance, into something better than the kind of world in which we now live— I cannot believe that a world society of order, of security, and of peace may not be realized, provided those responsible for its planning are willing to make the sacrifices required and are able to construct its foundations upon the rock of right, of justice, and of scientific truth, rather than upon the sands of selfishness, of compromise, and of expediency.

It is not idealism that is the danger to the community. Grave danger does lie in the all-too-frequent unwillingness of the idealist to grasp the hard facts of national and international experience; but it lies equally, in my judgment, in the defeatist philosophy of the cynic who, because of the failures of the past, cannot envision the successes of the future.

It will help us to keep our perspective if, from the vantage point of the present, we frequently look back over the list of errors of omission and of commission of the past. Let me make a few brief statements with regard to recent history which, I hope you will feel, as I do, should be regarded as axiomatic.

Trade—the exchange of goods—is inherently a matter of cooperation, but a glance at the past is enough to show that in the policies of nations this simple truism has been more often ignored than observed. Nations have more often than not undertaken economic discriminations and raised up trade barriers with complete disregard for the damaging effects on the trade and livelihood of other peoples and, ironically enough, with similar disregard for the harmful resultant effects upon their own export trade. They have considered foreign trade a cut-throat game in which each participant could only profit by taking undue advantage of his neighbor. Our own policy at times in the past has, as we all know, constituted no exception.

After the last war at a time when other countries were looking to us for help in their stupendous task of economic and social reconstruction, the United States, suddenly become the world's greatest creditor nation and incomparably strong economically, struck heavy blows at their war-weakened, debt-burdened, economic structures. The shock was heavy, morally as well as economically. The harmful effects of this policy on the trade, industry, and conditions of living of people of many other foreign countries were immediate. Our high-tariff policy reached out to virtually every corner of the earth and brought poverty and despair to innumerable communities.

But the effects on American importers, and on American industries dependent upon imports, were likewise immediate.

Unfortunately, the inevitable effects on our export trade were obscured and put off for a number of years by lavish foreign lending, both public and private. The most important normal source of foreign purchasing power for American exports—other countries' exports to us—was being dried up, but what was really happening, as we all know, was that countless American investors were in effect paying American exporters for billions of dollars' worth of goods sent abroad. If the deficiency in normal foreign purchasing power derived from sales in this country had not been covered up by such vast sums advanced by American investors, we might have realized much earlier that our tariff policy was striking at the very roots of our entire export trade. We might have avoided the colossal blunder of 1930 and the less serious, but equally misguided, action of further tariff increases under the guise of the so-called excise taxes of 1932. Many foreign countries, which had not recovered from the shock of our tariff increases in 1921 and 1922 and were tottering on the brink of economic and financial collapse, were literally pushed into the abyss by our tariff action of 1930. Throughout the world this withering blast of trade destruction brought disaster and despair to countless people.

The resultant misery, bewilderment, and resentment, together with other equally pernicious contributing causes, paved the way for the rise of those very dictatorships which have plunged almost the entire world into war.

When human beings see ahead of them nothing but a continuation of the distress of the present, they are not apt to analyze dispassionately the worth of the glittering assurance of better times held out to them by a self-styled leader whom they would under more normal circumstances recognize as the shoddy adventurer which in reality he proves to be.

We thus helped to set in motion a whirlpool of trade-restricting measures and devices, preferences, and discriminations, which quickly sucked world trade down to such low levels that standards of living everywhere were dangerously reduced. Faced with the disappearance of markets in the United States for so many of their exportable products, foreign countries were forced to cut their economic cloth accordingly. They erected high tariffs and established restrictive quotas designed to keep their imports of American products within the limits of their reduced dollar purchasing power. They sought desperately for other markets and other sources of supply. In the process they entered into all sorts of preferential arrangements, resorted to primitive barter, and adopted narrowly bilateralistic trade-and-payments arrangements.

Obviously the totalitarian governments then being set up seized avidly on the opportunity so afforded to undertake political pressures through the exercise of this form of commercial policy.

They substituted coercion for negotiation—"persuaded," with a blackjack. The countries thus victimized were forced to spend the proceeds of their exports in the countries where such proceeds were blocked, no matter how inferior the quality, how high the price, or even what the nature might be of the goods which they were thus forced to obtain. They were prevented by such arrangements from entering into beneficial trade agreements with countries unwilling to sanction discriminations against their exports. By no means the least of the victims were the exporters of third countries, including the United States, who were either shut out of foreign markets entirely or else only permitted to participate on unequal terms.

This time our own export trade, unsupported by foreign lending on the part of American investors and unprotected against countless new trade barriers and discriminations, was immediately disastrously affected. Belatedly we recognized our mistake. We realized that something had to be done to save our export trade from complete destruction.

The enactment in 1934 of the Trade Agreements Act represented a new deal for our foreign trade, a reorientation of government policy on the basis of simple, obvious facts, one of the most simple and obvious being that a nation cannot continue to sell if it does not buy. I do not need to dwell on this phase. You who are meeting here have recognized in repeated resolutions of endorsement the merits of that policy and the simple truths upon which it is founded.

To that policy history will always attach the honored name of Cordell Hull. But time is required for such a reversal of policy to have its full effects, and in the meantime another shattering world war has again laid the whole international economic structure in ruins and has enormously increased the task of reconstruction.

So much for the past.

For the people of this country the supreme objective of the present before which every other consideration must now give place is the final and complete defeat of Hitlerism. We have been forced in self-defense to assure ourselves that the ever-growing menace to our free institutions and to our national safety cannot and shall not prevail.

For that reason the trade problems of the immediate moment have largely become problems arising out of our national emergency. As such their solution is imperative. You who are living daily with these problems before you are the last people who need to be told in any detail what they are. The function of foreign trade under present conditions is largely one of supplying the defenders of human liberty with the means of their defense and of obtaining, despite the shortage of shipping, the materials needed in carrying out our own defense program and in supplying the needs of our consumers.

There is likewise the acute problem of the essential import needs of our sister Republics of this hemisphere which are largely cut off from European sources of supply. Far too little emphasis, I regret to say, has as yet been placed upon the vital obligation of this country to cooperate to a far greater practical extent than has as yet been the case in assisting to the fullest degree possible our neighbors of the Western Hemisphere in the maintenance of their own national economies in the ever-increasing dislocation to which they are subjected.

There is also need for additional trade agreements which will help during the emergency and which will assist in establishing a sound foundation for international trade after the war. Your Government intends to go forward with this program.

But the future no less than the present presses itself upon our attention. It seems to me that there is nothing more urgently demanded than that the people of the United States, the governments of the Western Hemisphere, and the governments of all of the nations which have been assailed or menaced by the Axis powers should daily be considering and determining upon the policies and practices whose future enforcement could render the greatest measure of assurance that the tragedy which we now see being unfolded should not once more be brought to pass.

I can conceive of no greater misfortune than that the people of the United States and their Government should refrain from devoting themselves to the study of reconstruction until the end of the war, than that they should permit themselves to adopt the passive policy of "wait and see."

The period following the present war will be fully as critical for us as is the present crisis. Forces of aggression now menace us from without. But dangers of another nature here and elsewhere will threaten us even after the war has ended in the victory of Great Britain and her allies over the powers that are seeking to place the whole of the world under their own ignominious form of tyranny.

There exists the danger, despite the clear lessons of the past, that the nations of the world will once more be tempted to resort to the same misguided policies which have had such disastrous consequences. And in the economic field especially there is danger that special interests and pressure groups in this country and elsewhere will once again selfishly and blindly seek preferences for themselves and discriminations against others.

The creation of an economic order in the post-war world which will give free play to individual enterprise, and at the same time render security to men and women and provide for the progressive improvement of living standards, is almost as essential to the preservation of free institutions as is the actual winning of this war. And the preservation of our liberties, all-important in itself, is essential to the realization of the other great objective of mankind—an enduring peace. There can be no peace in a Hitler-ridden world.

In brief, in my judgment the creation of that kind of sound economic order which I have described is essential to the attainment of those three great demands of men and women everywhere—freedom, security, and peace.

The stakes are therefore tremendous in the task to which we must earnestly set ourselves. All of the talent of such organizations as this great organization of yours, of research institutions, and of the agencies of government must be brought to bear upon the solution of the post-war economic problems.

These problems are of two kinds: those which will present themselves as the immediate aftermath of the war and those involved in the creation of a more permanent economic order.

In the immediate post-war period the task will primarily be one of reconstruction. Food and material of all kinds will be sorely needed. Both humanitarian considerations and self-interest require that we cooperate to these ends to the fullest extent of our ability. So long as any important part of the world is economically sick, we cannot be well.

Plans for meeting these requirements are already being considered. In planning commodity agreements for stabilizing prices of basic commodities, such as the wheat agreement now under consideration by several of the producing countries directly concerned, these unusual post-war needs must be kept in mind in order that adequate supplies may be available to meet them.

Both from the standpoint of immediate post-war needs and in the longer-range aspect, we must give serious attention to the problems of nutrition. Here again humanitarian considerations and self-interest combine to make this subject one of outstanding importance to our people. If the dietary needs of the world's population could be satisfied to the extent necessary to meet minimum standards for sustaining health, the burdensome surpluses which normally trouble producers of many staple products would disappear. I am glad to be able to assure you that this subject is being given preferential attention by agencies of this and other governments.

These are some of the problems with which we shall be faced immediately after the war. But the basic problem in establishing a new and better world order is to obtain

the application by the nations of the world of sound principles of commercial and economic policy.

The basic principles which, in my judgment, should
guide the policies of nations in the post-war world have
recently been enunciated in the eight-point joint declaration of the President and Mr. Churchill* at the historic
meeting of the Atlantic.

This set of basic principles, appropriately called "The
Atlantic Charter," deals with commercial policy in its
fourth point, which reads, "They will endeavor, with due
respect for their existing obligations, to further the enjoyment by all states, great or small, victor or vanquished, of access, on equal terms, to the trade and to
the raw materials of the world which are needed for their
economic prosperity."

This categorical statement of the essentials of post-war
commercial policy requires no interpretation. I should,
however, like to emphasize its meaning and significance.

The basic conception is that your Government is determined to move towards the creation of conditions under
which restrictive and unconscionable tariffs, preferences,
and discriminations are things of the past; under which
no nation should seek to benefit itself at the expense of
another; and under which destructive trade warfare shall
be replaced by cooperation for the welfare of all nations.

The Atlantic declaration means that every nation has
a right to expect that its legitimate trade will not be
diverted and throttled by towering tariffs, preferences,
discriminations, or narrow bilateral practices. Most fortunately we have already done much to put our own
commercial policy in order. So long as we adhere and per-

* *Department of State Bulletin,* August 16, 1941, p. 125.

sistently implement the principles and policies which made possible the enactment of the Trade Agreements Act, the United States will not furnish, as it did after the last war, an excuse for trade-destroying and trade-diverting practices.

The purpose so simply set forth in the Atlantic declaration is to promote the economic prosperity of all nations "great or small, victor or vanquished." Given this purpose and the determination to act in accordance with it, the means of attaining this objective will always be found. It is a purpose which does not have its origin primarily in altruistic conceptions. It is inspired by the realization, so painfully forced on us by the experiences of the past and of the present, that in the long run no nation can prosper by itself or at the expense of others and that no nation can live unto itself alone.

No nation's peace can be assured in the disordered world in which we have lived since 1914.

It is the task and responsibility of every one of us, and like-minded people everywhere, to see that our objective is attained. We cannot afford to repeat the tragic mistakes of the past.

Wilson and the
Atlantic Charter

TWENTY-THREE years ago today, Woodrow
Wilson addressed the Congress of the United States
in order to inform the representatives of the American
people of the terms of the Armistice which signalized the
victorious conclusion of the first World War.

That day marked, as he then said, the attainment of
a great objective: the opportunity for the setting up of
"such a peace as will satisfy the longing of the whole
world for disinterested justice, embodied in settlements
which are based upon something much better and much
more lasting than the selfish competitive interests of
powerful states."

Less than five years later, shrouded in the cerements
of apparent defeat, his shattered body was placed in the
grave beside which we now are gathered.

He was laid to rest amid the apathy of the many, and
amid the sneers of those of his opponents who had,
through appeal to ignorance, to passion, and to prejudice, temporarily persuaded the people of our country to
reject Wilson's plea that the influence, the resources, and
the power of the United States be exercised for their own
security and for their own advantage, through our par-

ticipation in an association of the free and self-governed peoples of the world.

And yet, when we reflect upon the course of the years that have since intervened, how rarely in human history has the vision of a statesman been so tragically and so swiftly vindicated. Only a score of years have since elapsed, and today the United States finds itself in far greater peril than it did in 1917. The waves of world conquest are breaking high both in the East and in the West. They are threatening, more nearly each day that passes, to engulf our own shores.

Beyond the Atlantic a sinister and pitiless conqueror has reduced more than half of Europe to abject serfdom. It is his boast that his system shall prevail even unto the ends of the earth. In the Far East the same forces of conquest under a different guise are menacing the safety of all nations that border upon the Pacific.

Were these forces to prevail, what place in such a world would there be for the freedoms which we cherish and which we are passionately determined to maintain?

Because of these perils we are arming ouselves to an extent to which we have never armed ourselves before. We are pouring out billions upon billions of dollars in expenditures, not only in order that we may successfully defend ourselves and our sister nations of the Western Hemisphere, but also, for the same ends, in order to make available the weapons of defense to Great Britain, to Russia, to China, and to all the other nations that have until now so bravely fought back the hordes of the invaders. And in so doing we are necessarily diverting the greater part of our tremendous productive capacity into channels of destruction, not those of construction, and we are piling up a debt burden which will inevitably affect the manner of life, and diminish the opportunity for progressive advancement, of our children and of our children's children.

But far graver than that—for the tides are running fast—our people realize that at any moment war may be forced upon us, and if it is, the lives of all of us will have to be dedicated to preserving the freedom of the United States and to safeguarding the independence of the American people, which are more dear to us than life itself.

The heart-searching question which every American citizen must ask himself on this day of commemoration is whether the world in which we have to live would have come to this desperate pass had the United States been willing in those years which followed 1919 to play its full part in striving to bring about a new world order based on justice and on "a steadfast concert for peace."

Would the burdens and the dangers which the American people might have had to envisage through that "partnership of democratic nations" which Woodrow Wilson then urged upon them, have represented even an infinitestimal portion of the burdens and the dangers with which they are now confronted?

Solely from the standpoint of the interest of the American people themselves, who saw straight and who thought straight twenty years ago? Was it Woodrow Wilson when he pleaded with his fellow Americans to insure the safety and the welfare of their country by utilizing the influence and the strength of their great nation in joining with the other peace-loving powers of the earth in preventing the outgrowth of those conditions which have made possible this new world upheaval? Or was it that group of self-styled "practical, hard-headed Americans" who jeered at his idealism, who loudly proclaimed that our very system of government would be destroyed if we raised our voice in the determination of world affairs, and who refused to admit that our security could be even remotely jeopardized if the whole of the rest of the earth was plunged into the chaos of world anarchy?

A cycle in human events is about to come to its end.

The American people after full debate, in accordance with their democratic institutions, have determined upon their policy. They are pledged to defend their freedom and their ancient rights against every form of aggression and to spare no effort and no sacrifice in bringing to pass the final defeat of Hitlerism and all that which that evil term implies. We have no doubt of the ultimate victory of the forces of liberty and of human decency. But we cannot know, we cannot yet foresee, how long and how hard the road may be which leads to that new day when another armistice will be signed.

And what will come to pass thereafter?

Three months ago the President of the United States and the Prime Minister of the United Kingdom signed and made public a new charter "on which they base their hopes for a better future for the world."

The principles and the objectives set forth in that joint declaration gave new hope and new courage to millions of people throughout the earth. They saw again more clearly the why and the wherefore of this ghastly struggle. They saw once more the gleam of hope on the horizon— hope for liberty, freedom from fear and want, the satisfaction of their craving for security.

These aspirations of human beings everywhere cannot again be defrauded. Those high objectives set forth in the Charter of the Atlantic must be realized. They must be realized, quite apart from every other consideration, because of the fact that the individual interest of every man and woman in the United States will be advanced consonantly with the measure in which the world where they live is governed by right and by justice and the measure in which peace prevails.

The American people thus have entered the Valley of Decision.

Shall we as the most powerful nation of the earth once more stand aloof from all effective and practical forms of international concert wherein our participation could in all human probability insure the maintenance of a peaceful world in which we can safely live? Can we afford again to refrain from lifting a finger until gigantic forces of destruction threaten all of modern civilization and the raucous voice of a criminal paranoiac, speaking as the spokesman for these forces from the cellar of a Munich beer hall, proclaims as his set purpose the destruction of our own security and the annihilation of religious liberty, of political liberty, and of economic liberty throughout the earth?

The decision rests solely with the people of the United States: the power is theirs to determine the kind of world of the future in which they would live. Is it conceivable that, in enlightened self-interest, they could once more spurn that opportunity?

When the time for the making of that great decision is at hand, I believe that they will turn again for light and for inspiration to the ideals of that great seer, statesman, patriot, and lover of his fellow men—Woodrow Wilson—whose memory we here today revere. Then again they will remember that great cause he once held up before their eyes: "A universal dominion of right by such a concert of free peoples as shall bring peace and safety to all nations and make the world itself at last free."

The Road before
the Americas

THE PEOPLES of the Americas face today the greatest danger which they have ever confronted since
they won their independence. We are meeting together
under the terms and in the spirit of inter-American agreements to take counsel as to the course which our governments should take under the shadow of this dire threat to
our continued existence as free peoples.

We meet as the representatives of nations which in
former times have had their differences and controversies. But I believe that I may speak for all of us, and not
least in the name of my own Government, when I say
that we all of us have learned by our past errors of omission and of commission. We are assembled as representatives of the twenty-one sovereign and independent Republics of the American continent, now welded together
as no continent has ever before been united in history,
by our faith in the ties of mutual trust and of reciprocal
interdependence which bind us and, most of all, by our
common devotion to the great cause of democracy and
of human liberty to which our New World is dedicated.

The calamity which has now engulfed humanity was
not unforeseen by any of us.

Just five years ago at the Inter-American Conference for the Maintenance of Peace of Buenos Aires, we met because of the clear signs that the earth would be engulfed by the tidal wave of a world-wide war. By common accord we determined upon measures indispensable to our common security. At the Inter-American Conference at Lima further measures were taken. After the war broke out, at the Meetings of the Foreign Ministers at Panama and Habana the American Republics adopted additional far-reaching measures of protection and of cooperation for their common safety. We were thus in many ways prepared for that eventuality from which we then still hoped we might be spared, the involvement of the Americas in the war which has been forced upon mankind by Hitlerism.

I regard it as my obligation here on behalf of my Government to inform you with complete frankness of the course which it had pursued up to the time when, on Sunday, December 7, my country was suddenly attacked by means of an act of treachery that will never be forgotten by the people of the United States nor, I believe, by the people of any of the other American Republics.

My Government was never blind to the ultimate purposes and objectives of Hitlerism. It long since realized that Hitler had formulated his plans to conquer the entire world. These plans—the plans of a criminal paranoiac— were conceived before he had even seized power in Germany. They have been carried out step by step, first through guile and deceit, later by fire and sword. No evil has been too monstrous for him. No infamy has been too vile for him to perpetrate.

Time and again, as you all know, the President of

the United States, with your knowledge and with your approval, made every effort in earlier years by fervent appeal and by constructive and just proposal to avert the final holocaust.

All of us learned a bitter lesson in those years between 1936 and 1941. We learned by the tragic experience of others that all of those standards of international decency and of international law, upon which the hopes of a law-abiding and a peaceful world were based, were utterly disregarded by Hitler and by his ignominious satellites.

Those free nations who sought ingenuously, by the very innocence of their conduct and by the very completeness of their neutrality, to maintain at least the shadow of their independence were occupied more promptly, and ravaged more cruelly, than those who resisted the attack of Hitler's armies.

We have been taught this lesson—which it took all of us a long time to learn—that in the world of today, confronted by Hitlerism and all of the black reversion to barbarism which that evil word implies, no nation can hope to maintain its own independence, and no people can hope to maintain its liberty, except through the power of armed might and through the courage and devotion of men and women who are of many lands and of many races, but who all of them love liberty more than life itself.

The people of the United States learned that lesson.

And for that reason, because of their determination to defend their country and to safeguard the security of our common continent, they determined to lend every form of assistance to that gallant band of nations who against great odds continued nevertheless to defend their own liberties.

We had learned our lesson so clearly that we saw that the defense by these peoples of their independence constituted likewise the defense of our own independence and of that of the Western Hemisphere.

Then suddenly last June, Hitler, distraught by the realization that he could no longer attempt successfully to invade Great Britain, but intoxicated by the easy victories which he had achieved in other parts of Europe, perfidiously attacked the Soviet Union, with which he had only recently entered into a pact of nonaggression.

"Whom the gods would destroy, they first make mad."

Many months ago Japan entered into the Tripartite Pact with Germany and Italy. My Government learned that this arrangement, which made of Japan the submissive tool of Hitler for the primary purpose of preventing the United States from continuing to give assistance to Great Britain, was not supported by certain elements in Japan. These elements clearly foresaw the ultimate destruction of Japan if the Japanese Government dared to embark upon an adventure which would ultimately bring Japan into conflict with all of the other powers which had direct interests in the Western Pacific. These elements in Japan also realized that, while Hitler had been able to inveigle the war lords in control of the Japanese Government into believing that should Japan carry out German orders, and were the Western democracies defeated, Germany would permit Japan to control the Far East, Hitler would of course take her spoils from Japan whenever he saw fit.

[37]

My Government sought over a period of more than ten months to negotiate with Japan a peaceful and equitable adjustment of differences between the two countries so as to prevent the outbreak of war in the Pacific.

The United States, however, utterly refused to agree to any settlement which would infringe upon the independence or the legitimate rights of the people of China who for four and a half years had been bravely and successfully resisting every effort on the part of Japan to conquer their ancient land. Nor would the United States agree to any proposal offered by the Japanese Government which would contravene those basic principles of right and justice for which, I am proud to say, my country stands.

We now know that at the very time that the present Japanese Government was carrying on, at its own urgent request, the pretense of conducting peaceful negotiations with the United States for the purpose of reaching a settlement which would have averted war, every plan in its uttermost detail had already been made to attack my country's territory. During those last two weeks before December 7, when Japan's notorious peace emissary was protesting to my Government that his country desired nothing except peace and profitable commercial relations with the United States, the airplane carriers were already on their way to Pearl Harbor to launch their dastardly attack upon the United States Navy.

The Japanese war lords, under the orders of their German masters, adopting the same methods of deceit and treachery which Hitler has made a stench in the nostrils of civilized mankind, while peace negotiations were actually still in progress in Washington, suddenly attacked a country which had been Japan's friend and which had made every honorable effort to find a basis for a just and lasting peace in the Pacific.

A few days later Germany and her satellites declared war upon the United States.

And so war has been forced upon some of us in the American continent.

The greatest assurance that our great association of sovereign and independent peoples—the American family of nations—can survive this world upheaval safely lies in the unity with which we face the common peril.

Some of us by our own power, by our own resources, by the extent of our population, are able successfully beyond the shadow of a doubt to defend ourselves. Others of us who do not possess these material advantages, equal though they be in their courage and in their determination to resist aggression, must depend for their continued security upon the cooperation which other members of the American family may give them. The only assured safety which this continent possesses lies in full cooperation between us all in the common defense: equal and sovereign partners in times of aggression as in times of peace.

The record of the past two years is ever before us. You and I know that had there existed during the past decade an international order based upon law, and with the capacity to enforce such law, the earth today would not be subjected to the cruel scourge which is now ravaging the entire globe. Had the law-abiding and peaceful nations of Europe been willing to stand together when the menace of Hitlerism first began to become manifest, Hitler would never have dared to embark upon his evil course. It was solely because of the fact that these nations, instead of standing together, permitted themselves to hold aloof one from the other and placed their hope of salvation in their own neutrality, that Hitler was enabled to overrun them one by one as time and circumstances made it expedient for him.

The security of the three hundred millions of people who inhabit the Western Hemisphere and the independence of each of the countries here represented will be determined by whether the American nations stand together in this hour of peril or whether they stand apart one from the other.

I am fully aware of what the representatives of the Axis powers have been stating to some of you, day in and day out during the past months. I know that Hitler's representatives have said to some of you that Germany has not the slightest thought of dominating the Western Hemisphere. All that Germany wants, they have told you, is complete domination over every part of Europe, of Africa, and of the Near East, the destruction of the British Empire, the enslavement of the Russian people, the overlordship of the Far East, and when this is accomplished, only friendship and peaceful trade with the Americas.

But Hitler's representatives have omitted to mention that in such a fateful contingency we would all of us then also be living in a Hitler-dominated world. You may remember that a few days ago Hitler publicly denounced President Roosevelt as the greatest warmonger of all time because the President had declared that the people of the United States "did not want to live in the type of world" that Hitler wished for. In a Hitler-dominated universe not one of us could trade except on Hitler's terms. Not one of us could live except under a gauleiter appointed for us by Hitler. Not one of us could educate our children except as Hitler dictated. Not one of us could enjoy our God-given rights to think and to speak freely and to worship the Deity as our conscience may dictate.

Can even Hitler wonder that we are not willing to live in such a world as that?

I know what representatives of Japan have been saying to some of you. They are telling you that the Japanese Government is sure that the governments and peoples of the American Republics will certainly not be influenced by any thought that Japan may harbor ulterior motives towards them. They are telling you that Japan desires nothing but peace with you and the maintenance of profitable commercial relations.

You will remember that they told us that also!

The Japanese Government is even telling you that they are soon going to send ships to the Pacific ports of South America to take cargoes of your goods. But they did not add that were some Japanese ship to be foolhardy enough to attempt to make such a trip, it would not be able to travel many miles after leaving the port of the Americas to which it had gone, except under the naval custody of Japan's adversaries.

But there is no useful purpose to be served by our dwelling on the lies with which the Axis governments still attempt to deceive us. We all of us know that no sane man can place the slightest shred of credence in any solemn or sworn assurance which the Axis governments give.

We likewise know full well that the sole aim, the ultimate objective of these partners in crime, is conquest of the surface of the entire earth, the loot of the possessions of every one of us, and the subjugation of free men and women everywhere to the level of serfs.

Twelve months ago Hitler solemnly assured the German people that before the end of the year 1941 Germany would complete the defeat of all her enemies in the greatest victory of all time. On October 3 last Hitler swore to his people that before the first of the new year of 1942 Russia would be crushed, "never to rise again."

What are the facts? Today the German armies are retreating from Russian territory, routed and dispersed by the magnificent offensive of the Russian armies. Hitler has lost over one-third of his air force, over one-half of his tank force, and more than three million men. But more than that, the German people now see for themselves the utter falsity of the promises held out to them by the evil charlatan who rules them. Their morale is running low.

In North Africa the British armies have utterly destroyed the Axis forces in Libya and are clearing the Southern Mediterranean littoral of Axis threats. In the Atlantic the British and United States convoys are moving ever more safely to their destinations, and the loss of merchant shipping through German submarine action has steadily diminished during the past six months.

In the Far East the United States and Great Britain have met with initial reverses.

We all remember that as a result of the Washington Limitation of Armaments Conference of 1922 the powers directly interested in the Far East, in order to assure the basis for peaceful relations between them, pledged themselves not to increase the fortifications of their possessions in that area. During all of the years that the Treaties agreed upon at that Conference remained in effect, the United States consequently took no steps to fortify the Philippines. But we also now know that, counter to her sworn obligations, Japan during these same years was creating naval bases and feverishly constructing fortifications throughout the islands of the South Seas which she had received as a mandate from the League of Nations.

Furthermore, at the request of the Philippine people the Government of the United States had pledged itself to grant full independence to them in the year 1946.

The infamous attack by Japan upon the United States consequently found the Philippine Islands largely unfortified and protected solely by a modest army of brave Filipino soldiers, supported by only two divisions of United States troops, with a small air force utterly inadequate to withstand the concentrated strength of the Japanese.

But the control of the Pacific Ocean itself rests with the Allied fleets. Japan after suffering disastrously in her four-year-long war with China is surrounded on all sides. She possesses no resources. Once the materiel which she is now using is destroyed, it can only be replaced by what Japan herself can produce. And that replacement will be inferior in quality and small in quantity without the raw materials which Japan will now be largely unable to secure.

The commencement of the year 1942 has marked the turn of the tide. The United States is now in the war. Our industrial production, the greatest in the world, is fast mounting towards the maximum. During the coming year we will produce some 60,000 airplanes, including 45,000 military airplanes, some 45,000 tanks, some 300 new combatant ships, from the mightiest battleships to coastal patrol craft, and some 600 new merchant ships. We will attain a rate of 70,000 per year in the training of combat airplane pilots. We have drafted for military service all of our men between the ages of 20 and 44 years, and of this great total we will soon have an initial army of 3,000,000 men fully trained and fully equipped. We will spend 50 billions of dollars, or half of our total national income, in the year thereafter in order to secure the use of every ounce of our national resources in our war effort. Every weapon that we produce will be used wherever it is determined that it may be of the most service in the common cause—whether that be here in the Western Hemisphere, on the deserts of Libya, on the steppes of Russia, or in the territory of the brave people of China.

Those of us who have joined in this holy war face a ruthless and barbarous foe. The road before us will be hard and perhaps long. We will meet unquestionably with serious reverses from time to time. But the tide has turned, and will run swiftly and ever more swiftly until it ends in the flood of victory.

As each one of you knows, my Government has made no suggestion and no request as to the course which any of the governments of the other American Republics should pursue subsequent to the Japanese attack upon the United States and the declaration of war upon it by the other Axis powers. We do not function in that way in the American family of nations.

But may I assure you from my heart today that the spontaneous declaration of war upon the enemies of mankind of nine of the other American Republics; the severance of all relations with Germany, Italy, and Japan by

Mexico, Colombia, and Venezuela; and the official declarations of solidarity and support by all of the other American Republics, including our traditional and unfailing friend in evil days as well as good, the great Republic of Brazil, whose guests we all are today, represent to my Government and to my fellow citizens a measure of support, of strength, and of spiritual encouragement which no words of mine would be adequate to express.

May I merely say that these acts of faith in our common destiny, so generously realized, will never be forgotten by the people of the United States. They have heartened us all. They have made us all the more anxious to be worthy—not in words but in deeds—of your confidence. They have made us all the more desirous of showing our gratitude through the extent of the cooperative strength which we can furnish to insure the ultimate triumph of the cause to which we are dedicated.

Each one of the American governments has determined and will continue to determine in its own wisdom the course which it will pursue to the best interest of its people in this world struggle. But of one thing I feel sure we are all convinced. In accordance with the obligations we have all undertaken under the provisions of our inter-American agreements and in accordance with the spirit of that continental solidarity unanimously proclaimed, those nations of the Americas which are not engaged in war will never permit their territory to be used by agents of the Axis powers in order that these may conspire against, or prepare attacks upon, those Republics which are fighting for their own liberties and for those of the entire continent.

We all of us are fully aware of the record of the activities of Axis agents in our several countries which the past two years have brought to light. We know how the Axis diplomatic representatives, taking advantage of the immunity which international custom has granted them for their legitimate functions, have been doing their utmost to poison inter-American relations, to create internal discord and to engender domestic strife, so as to try and pave the way for subversive movements financed with funds obtained through extortion from residents in our midst or transferred from the loot they have procured in the occupied countries of Europe. We know that their so-called consular officials have in reality been the directing heads of espionage rings in every part of this hemisphere. The full history of this record will some day be published in full detail when the divulging of this information will no longer be of assistance to the enemy.

So long as this hemisphere remained out of the war, all of our governments dealt with this ever-increasing danger in the manner which they believed most effective, exchanging intelligence one with the other as existing agreements between them provide whenever such exchange was mutually helpful.

But today the situation has changed. Ten of the American Republics are at war and three others have severed all relations with the Axis powers. The continued presence of these Axis agents within the Western Hemisphere constitutes a direct danger to the national defense of the Republics engaged in war. There is not a Japanese nor a German consul, nor a consul of Hitler's satellite countries, in the New World at this moment who is not reporting to his superiors every time a ship leaves the ports of the country where he is stationed, for the purpose of having that ship sunk by an Axis submarine. There is not a diplomatic representative of the Axis powers anywhere in the Americas who is not seeking to get for his masters information regarding the defense preparations of the American nations now at war, who is not conspiring against the internal security of every one of us, who is not doing his utmost through every means available to him to hinder our capacity to insure the integrity of our freedom and our independence.

Surely this danger must be of paramount concern to all of us. The preeminent issue presented is solely that those Republics engaged in war shall not be dealt a deadly thrust by the agents of the Axis ensconced upon the soil, and enjoying the hospitality, of others of the American Republics.

The shibboleth of classic neutrality in its narrow sense can, in this tragic modern world, no longer be the ideal of any freedom-loving people of the Americas. There can no longer be any real neutrality as between the powers of evil and the forces that are struggling to preserve the rights and the independence of free peoples. It is far better for any people to strive gloriously to safeguard its independence; it is far better for any people to die, if need be, in the battle to save its liberties, than by clinging to the tattered fiction of an illusory neutrality, succeed only by so doing in committing suicide.

Our devotion to the common cause of defending the New World against aggression does not imply necessarily engagement in war. But it does imply, I confidently believe, the taking of all measures of cooperation between us which redound to the great objective of keeping the Americas free.

Of equal importance with measures of political solidarity, defense cooperation, and the repression of subversive activity are economic measures related to the conduct of war against the aggressor nations and the defense of the Western Hemisphere.

All of the American Republics have already taken some form of measures breaking off financial and commercial intercourse between them and the non-American aggressor states and to eliminate other alien economic activities prejudicial to the welfare of the American Republics. It is of the utmost importance that these measures be expanded in order that they may prevent all business, financial, and trade transactions between the Western Hemisphere and the aggressor states and all transactions within the Western Hemisphere which directly or indirectly redound to the benefit of the aggressor nations or are in any way inimical to the defense of the hemisphere.

The conduct of war and the defense of the hemisphere will require an ever-increasing production of the implements of war and an ever-increasing supply of the basic and strategic materials necessary for their production. The spread of the war has cut off many of the most important sources of strategic materials, and it is essential that the American Republics conserve their stocks of such commodities and by every possible means encourage the production and the free flow within the hemisphere of the greatest possible quantity of these materials.

The universal character of the war is placing increasing demands upon the merchant-shipping facilities of all of us. The increased production of strategic materials will be of no avail unless adequate transportation can be provided, and it is consequently of vital importance that all of the shipping facilities of the Americas be mobilized to this essential end.

The Government of the United States is prepared to cooperate wholeheartedly with the other American Republics in handling the problems arising out of these economic warfare measures. It stands prepared to render financial and technical assistance where needed to alleviate injury to the domestic economy of any of the American Republics which results from the control and curbing of alien economic activities inimical to our common defense. It is ready to enter into broad arrangements for the acquisition of supplies of basic and strategic materials and to cooperate with each of the other American Republics in order to increase rapidly and efficiently their production for emergency needs. Finally, it stands ready through the United States Maritime Commission to render every assistance in the efficient operation of merchant vessels in accordance with the plan of August 28, 1941, of the Inter-American Financial and Economic Advisory Committee.

My Government is also fully aware of the important role which imported materials and articles play in the maintenance of the economies of your nations. On December 5, 1941, I advised the Inter-American Financial and Economic Advisory Committee in Washington that the United States was making every effort consistent with the defense program to maintain a flow to the other American Republics of materials to satisfy the minimum essential import requirements of your economies. I added that the policy of my Government was being interpreted by all of the appropriate agencies as calling for

[49]

recognition of and provision for the essential needs of the American Republics equal to the treatment accorded United States civilian needs.

The attack by Japan and the declarations of war by the other members of the Tripartite Pact have resulted in greater and unprecedented demands upon our production facilities. But I am able to state today as I did on the fifth of December that the policy of the United States toward the satisfaction of your essential requirements remains firm.

On December 26, 1941, after the outbreak of war the Board of Economic Warfare of my Government resolved unanimously: "It is the policy of the Government of the United States to aid in maintaining the economic stability of the other American Republics by recognizing and providing for their essential civilian needs on the basis of equal and proportionate consideration with our own."

Pursuant to this declaration of policy our allocation of 218,600 tons of tin plate for your needs during this year has been followed by further allocations which I am privileged to announce today. The Office of Production Management has advised me that allocations have been made to you for the next quarter, in amounts adequate to meet your needs for rayon; for twenty essential agricultural and industrial chemicals, including copper sulphate, ammonium sulphate, soda ash, and caustic soda; for farm equipment; and for iron and steel products.

In addition I am able to announce that a special mechanism has been organized within the Office of Production Management which is now facilitating the clearance of your individual priority applications.

In the light of this action, it seems appropriate to recognize that the arsenal of democracy continues mindful of its hemisphere responsibilities.

I am confident that your people will join the people of the United States, who are sharing their civilian supplies with you, in recognizing that military and other defense needs must continue to be given precedence over civilian demands.

All of these economic measures relate directly to the conduct of war, the defense of the hemisphere, and the maintenance of the economies of our several nations during the war emergency. Obviously our greatest efforts must be extended towards victory. Nevertheless, the full consummation of victory must include the building of an economic and social order in which all of our citizens may subsequently enjoy the blessings of peace.

My Government believes that we must begin now to execute plans, vital to the human defense of the hemisphere, for the improvement of health and sanitary conditions, the provision and maintenance of adequate supplies of food, milk, and water, and the effective control of insect-borne and other communicable diseases. The United States is prepared to participate in and to encourage complementary agreements among the American Republics for dealing with these problems of health and sanitation by provision, according to the abilities of the countries involved, of funds, raw materials, and services.

The responsibility with which we are all charged requires that we plan for broad economic and social development, for increased production of the necessities of the world, and for their equitable distribution among the people.

If this economic rehabilitation of the world is to take

place, it is indispensable that there be a resurgence of international trade—international trade, as was declared by the Second Meeting of Ministers of Foreign Affairs at Habana, "conducted with peaceful motives and based upon equality of treatment and fair and equitable practices."

I urge upon you all the imperative need for unity between us, not only in the measures which must presently be taken in the defense of our Western World, but also in order that the American Republics, joined as one, may prove to be the potent factor which they should be of right in the determination of the nature of the world of the future, after the victory is won.

We, the American nations, are trustees for Christian civilization. In our own relationships we have wished to show scrupulous respect for the sovereign rights of all states, we have sought to undertake only peaceful processes in the solution of controversies which may have arisen between us, and we have wished to follow the course of decency and of justice in our dealings with others.

When peace is restored, it is to the interest of the whole world that the American Republics present a united front and be able to speak and act with the moral authority to which, by reason of their own enlightened standards as much as by reason of their number and their power, they are entitled. The prayer of peoples throughout the world is that when the task of peace-making is once more undertaken it will be better done than it was in 1919. And we cannot forget that the task this time will be infinitely more difficult than it was the last time. In the determination of how these stupendous problems may best be solved, the united voice of the free peoples of the Americas must be heard.

The ideals which men have cherished have always throughout the course of history proved themselves to be more potent than any other factor. Nor conquest, nor migrations; nor economic pressure, nor pestilence; nor revolt, nor assassinations have ever yet been able to triumph over the ideals which have sprung from men's hearts and men's minds.

Notwithstanding the hideous blunders of the past generation, notwithstanding the holocaust of the present moment, that great ideal of "a universal dominion of right by such a concert of free peoples as shall bring peace and safety to all nations and make the world itself at last free" still stands untarnished as the supreme objective of a suffering humanity.

That ideal will yet triumph.

We, the free peoples of the Americas, must play our full part in its realization so that we may hasten the day when we can thus insure the maintenance of a peaceful world in which we, and our children, and our children's children, can safely live.

At this time the issue is clearly drawn. There can be no peace until Hitlerism and its monstrous parasites are utterly obliterated and until the Prussian and Japanese militarists have been taught in the only language they can understand that they will never again be afforded the opportunity of wrecking the lives of generation upon generation of men and women in every quarter of the globe.

When that time comes, men of good will must be prepared and ready to build with vision afresh upon new and lasting foundations of liberty, of morality, of justice, and, by no means least perhaps, of intelligence.

In the attainment of that great achievement the measure of our devotion will be the measure of the world's regeneration.

Joint Action in the Americas

MAY I express first of all my deep gratification at being afforded once again the privilege of being the guest of the Cuban Chamber of Commerce in the United States. For I am given in this way the satisfaction of meeting many of my Cuban friends and of feeling, during the hours I am with them, that I am closer to that great nation where I had the honor of representing this Government nine years ago.

It is all the more appropriate, therefore, for me tonight to render a deeply felt tribute of admiration and of gratitude to the people of Cuba and to their present Government. Cuba, as always, has proved loyal to her friendship and to her traditional ties with the United States. Those ties were consecrated in 1898. When this country was forced into war in 1917, Cuba again stood at her side. And now that the United States, through an act of cowardly aggression which will never be forgotten by the people of the United States, nor, I believe, by the peoples of any of the American Republics, has been forced into the greatest war of all times against the enemies of all that civilized man holds most dear, the Cuban people again, without hesitation or delay, have risen as one man to defend their own independence and the integrity of the Western Hemisphere and, by so doing, have come to the support of the United States.

Friendship of that magnitude is beyond praise. But I know that I speak for all of the American people when I say that their grateful recognition will be enduring.

During the brief period between January 15 and January 28, the world witnessed in the city of Rio de Janeiro the ending of an epoch in the Western Hemisphere and the beginning of a new era. It witnessed the termination of the period in the history of the Americas in which the phrase "the solidarity of the American Republics" had been an aspiration—a collection of mere words. There has now commenced a period of New World history in which inter-American solidarity has become a real, a living, and a vital truth.

The American foreign ministers met scarcely more than a month after Pearl Harbor. The war had been brought to America. They met fully conscious in many instances of the relatively undefended state of their own countries. They met under no illusions as to the nature of the struggle into which the world has now been plunged and well aware of the cruelty, the power, and the unlimited ambitions for conquest of the Axis powers.

But to them all, the fundamental issues were clear. They realized that in the course which destiny has traced for our New World there now existed for us all but two alternatives: either supine acquiescence in the plans which Hitler has charted for the enslavement of the freedom-loving peoples of the Americas, or else an immediate and resolute defiance of the would-be conqueror and the prompt taking of drastic and concerted measures for the common safety of all of the American Republics. They knew that the latter alternative meant victory and future security.

Unanimously the twenty-one American Republics determined upon their course. And the nature of their course was forthright and categorical. I can assure you that if the spirit of appeasement lingers anywhere on the American continent, it was not much in evidence at Rio de Janeiro. I shall read you the text of the first resolution agreed upon by the conference entitled "Breaking of Diplomatic Relations":

I

The American Republics reaffirm their declaration to consider any act of aggression on the part of a non-American State against one of them as an act of aggression against all of them, constituting as it does an immediate threat to the liberty and independence of America.

II

The American Republics reaffirm their complete solidarity and their determination to cooperate jointly for their mutual protection until the effects of the present aggression against the Continent have disappeared.

III

The American Republics, in accordance with the procedures established by their own laws and in conformity with the position and circumstances obtaining in each country in the existing continental conflict, recommend the breaking of their diplomatic relations with Japan, Germany and Italy, since the first-mentioned State attacked and the other two declared war on an American country.

IV

Finally, the American Republics declare that, prior to the reestablishment of the relations referred to in the preceding paragraph, they will consult among themselves in order that their action may have a solidary character.

Before the holding of the Conference at Rio de Janeiro, ten of the American Republics had declared war upon the Axis powers and three others, the Governments of Mexico, Colombia, and Venezuela, had already severed diplomatic relations with the enemy. Before the termination of the Conference and as soon as the resolution I have just read to you had been adopted, the Governments of Peru, of Uruguay, of Bolivia, of Paraguay, of Ecuador, and of Brazil likewise severed their diplomatic relations. It is true that as yet the Governments of Chile and of Argentina have not acted upon the recommendation in which they themselves joined, but, to paraphrase the eloquent metaphor of that great orator and statesman, the Foreign Minister of Mexico, Dr. Ezequiel Padilla, which he employed in the closing session of the Conference at Rio de Janeiro, in the firmament over the Western Hemisphere the stars of Argentina and Chile will surely soon be shining at the side of the stars of the other nineteen American Republics.

The Conference was in every sense a conference of acts and not a conference of words.

The American governments there agreed, likewise unanimously, upon the severance of all commercial and financial relations between the American Republics and the Axis powers. They agreed upon far-reaching measures of cooperation for mutual defense; for the maintenance through mutual assistance of the internal economy of the American Republics; for the stimulation and expansion of the production of strategic materials; for the mobilization of inter-American transportation facilities; for joint action in the most effective and detailed manner so as to eliminate subversive activities within the Americas; for the elimination of all Axis influence, direct or indirect, in the realm of radio and telephone and in the field of aviation; and finally, for joint action in preparation for the time when the victory shall have been won, so that the enlightened principles of decency, of humanity, of tolerance, and of understanding which have made our New World what it is today shall likewise be the determining principles in the shaping of the world of the future.

The negotiations at the Conference were undertaken in the true spirit of democracy. Some of us would have preferred in one or two instances the adoption of different methods of approach to the problems we had before us. But in every case an harmonious and unanimous agreement was had, which in no wise weakened the practical results we all sought. And thereby the great objective, the maintenance of the unity of the Americas, was preserved and strengthened.

I cannot fail tonight to express once more the gratitude all of us who attended the meeting had reason to feel because of the unfailing support given to the delegates in the achievement of their purposes by that wise and courageous statesman, the President of Brazil, and by his great Minister for Foreign Affairs, Dr. Aranha, who served as our Chairman.

Nor can I fail to emphasize the conspicuous and constructive part played in our deliberations by the representative of Cuba, Ambassador Concheso. Cuba was represented in her own best tradition. I can offer no higher tribute.

While technically it did not come within the scope of

the agenda before the Conference, the agreement reached at Rio de Janeiro between the Governments of Ecuador and of Peru for the final settlement of their century-and-a-quarter-old dispute will always be regarded as a direct result of the spirit engendered at that meeting. As you all know, that long-standing controversy had time and again given rise to the most serious difficulties between those two neighboring Republics. Tragically enough it had even resulted in actual hostilities last year. It had for generations thwarted and handicapped the prosperous development and the peaceful stability of the two nations involved. Its continuation had jeopardized the well-being of the entire hemisphere. I am happy to say that since the signing of the agreement the arrangements provided therein have been scrupulously carried out by both parties thereto, and it is the hope of all of us that the remaining and final steps will be taken in the immediate future so that this last remaining important controversy in our hemisphere may be regarded as finally liquidated.

I sometimes wonder if the people of the United States fully appreciate in the bitter struggle in which they are now engaged the significance to their own security of the striking demonstration of friendship and of support for them and for their cause which they have now been offered by their neighbors in the New World.

How different would our situation be today if on our southern border there lay a Republic of Mexico filled with resentment and with antagonism against the United States, instead of a truly friendly and cooperative Mexican people seeking the same objectives as ours, guided by the same policies, and inspired by the same motives, in their determination to safeguard their independence and the security of the hemisphere, as those which we ourselves possess; or if in those Republics more nearly adjacent to the Panama Canal there still burned a flaming hostility towards our Government because of acts of unjustifiable and unjustified intervention and of military occupation; or if the great Republics to the south were still deeply suspicious of our ultimate aims and outraged because of our unwillingness to concede their sovereign equality.

But if we look back a short decade ago, the picture I have just drawn will indicate the situation as it then existed. In this new gigantic war, were we confronted by conditions within the hemisphere as they then obtained, we would today be indeed gravely in danger. But fortunately, and we can never afford to forget it, there lives today throughout the length and breadth of the hemisphere a realization of community of interest, a recognition of American interdependence, which will prove to be the salvation of the New World and which renders full assurance that the liberties and the independence of the free peoples of the Americas will be maintained against all hazards and against all odds.

The bedrock upon which this new epoch of inter-American understanding is founded is the recognition in fact as well as in word that every one of the twenty-one American Republics is the sovereign equal of the others. That implies that interference by any one of them in the internal affairs of the others is inconceivable. Destroy or change that foundation and the inter-American federation which now exists will crash into ruins.

During recent months a strangely paradoxical situation has been increasingly frequently brought to my attention. Certain individuals and groups in the United States—who allege that they are representative of extreme liberal thought—have been publicly complaining that the policy of the Government of the United States in its dealings during these latter years with the other American Republics should have been a policy of open condemnation of existing governments in the other American nations, of a refusal of all forms of cooperation with those governments, and of open support of individuals or groups in those countries who happen to hold political views or beliefs which these critics regard as desirable. One of these gentlemen, a professor, in fact, in a book which he has recently published, has even gone so far as to maintain in the most portentous manner that this Government has been gravely derelict because it has not pursued in the Western Hemisphere what he terms a policy of "revolutionary democracy."

It is clear that what is here proposed is that the Government of the United States, by pressure, by bribery, by corruption, presumably even by open intervention, should have assisted in the overthrow of the established governments of the other American Republics in every case where they did not meet the requirements of this group of alleged liberals, so that they might be replaced with hand-picked governments of a different color. And I have no doubt that this group of alleged liberals would have been glad to do the picking for our Government!

The paradox lies in the fact that some of these persons are the very same individuals who only a generation ago were leading the fight with courage and with determination and with ultimate success to obtain from the Government of the United States the pursuit of a policy of nonintervention. I wonder if this group of alleged liberals to whom I refer has ever realized that what they are now proposing is the pursuit by their Government of a policy which is identical with that which has been pursued during the past five years by Hitler. What they are demanding in fact is the exercise by the United States of its power and of its influence in order to create puppet governments in the sovereign nations of the Western Hemisphere because of the belief by these people that these puppet governments would be more responsive to the political theories which they themselves hold.

But whether these misguided citizens of ours realize this truth or not, of one thing I am everlastingly sure, and that is that if the Government of the United States ever again undertakes within the New World a policy which constitutes interference, direct or indirect, in the domestic political concerns of our neighbors, the day when that policy is undertaken marks the end of all friendship and understanding between the American peoples. It would signalize the termination of the new epoch which commenced at Rio de Janeiro. It would mark the collapse of the finest and most practical form of international cooperation—the system of the Western Hemisphere—which in my judgment modern civilization has yet produced.

As between the two forces battling in this world upheaval which is now in process, and of which the gravity is increasing day by day, there is no longer any neutrality known to our New World. There is no government in the Americas which is neutral in its acts or in its policies. There are no peoples of the Americas who are neutral in thought or in sympathy. The Americas have unanimously cast their lot on the side of those who are fighting to save mankind from having to endure the darkness which would engulf it were Hitlerism to triumph.

All through the world, in every continent, in every quarter of the globe, men and women are laying down their lives in order to save the independence of their nations. To them the greatest sacrifice is not too great, if by the making of it they can insure that their children, and their fellows, can be free, free to worship God, free to think and to speak, and free to live out their lives in safety and in peace.

Thirty-seven governments, and thirty-seven peoples, today, in one form or another, have taken their stand in opposition to the Axis powers and in detestation of the cruel barbarism which these evil forces represent. They are joined in a common cause. Differing as they do in race, in color, in creed, in language, and in form of government, they are yet as one in their prayer for the victory of the principles of Christian civilization. For they realize that without a complete and crushing and permanent defeat of Hitlerism not one nation, not one Government, not one individual, can have any hope for the future.

Every foot of ground that the gallant Soviet armies regain from Hitler's troops constitutes a gain for us all. Every defeat inflicted upon the assassins of Japan by the brave forces of China is a blow at the tyranny which we are all determined must be defeated. Every set-back suffered by Hitler's satellites at the hands of the United Nations is that much new advantage to the cause which the peoples of these thirty-seven nations uphold.

Prejudices and antagonisms between us—stale but festering grievances of the past—wherever they still exist among these companions in this new crusade, must go by the board. There is no place any longer for any factor which hinders our common effort. There is only one issue today: it is to win the war.

Upon us, the people of the United States, are fixed the eyes of millions upon millions who have for long past been suffering the burden and heat of the battle. For many weary months they have been waging our fight for us. They now look to us to make good the faith they have in us. We cannot fail.

But we must immediately become fully conscious of our responsibility. We must at once attain the full measure of that achievement which is imperative to gain the victory.

We shall not fail.

We shall not fail because the end for which we strive, and which we seek, is that goal which to all the Americas, from Tierra del Fuego to Hudson's Bay, implies the one supreme value in life—Liberty.

The Realization of a Great Vision

TODAY as our nation faces the gravest danger it has ever confronted since it gained its independence, the American people are once more meeting together in every State of the Union to commemorate the observance of Memorial Day. In the elm-shaded churchyards of the New England hills, in the more newly consecrated burial places of the West, here in the quiet century-old cemeteries of the South, men and women throughout the land are now paying tribute to the memories of those who have made the ultimate sacrifice for their country and for their fellow men.

Eighty years ago our people were engaged in a fratricidal war between the States. In the fires of that devastating struggle was forged the great assurance that within the boundaries of the United States, men were, and would remain, free. The lives of those who died in that contest were not laid down in vain.

Forty-four years ago the United States went to war to help the gallant people of Cuba free themselves from the imposition by a nation of the Old World of a brutal tyranny which could not be tolerated in a New World dedicated to the cause of liberty. Through our victory in that war there was wrought a lasting safeguard to the independence of the Republics of the Western Hemisphere. Our citizens who then gave up their lives did not do so in vain.

Twenty-five years ago the United States declared war upon Germany. Our people went to war because of their knowledge that the domination of the world by German militarism would imperil the continuation of their national existence. We won that victory. Ninety thousand of our fellow Americans died in that great holocaust in order to win that victory. They died firm in the belief that the gift of their lives which they offered their country would be utilized by their countrymen as they had been promised it would be—to insure beyond doubt the future safety of the United States, through the creation of that kind of world in which a peaceful democracy such as ours could live in happiness and in security.

These ninety thousand dead, buried here on the slopes of Arlington and in the fields of France where they fell in battle, fulfilled their share of the bargain struck. Can we, the living, say as much? Can we truly say on this Memorial Day that we have done what we as a nation could have done to keep faith with them and to prevent their sacrifice from being made in vain?

The people of the United States were offered at the conclusion of the last war the realization of a great vision. They were offered the opportunity of sharing in the assumption of responsibility for the maintenance of peace in the world by participating in an international organization designed to prevent and to quell the outbreak of war. That opportunity they rejected. They rejected it in part because of the human tendency after a great upsurge of emotional idealism to seek the relapse into what was

once termed "normalcy." They rejected it because of
partisan politics. They rejected it because of the false
propaganda, widely spread, that by our participation in
a world order we would incur the danger of war rather
than avoid it. They rejected it because of unenlightened
selfishness.

At the dawn of the nineteenth century an English poet
wrote of his own land:

> she is a fen
> Of stagnant waters: altar, sword, and pen,
> Fireside, the heroic wealth of hall and bower,
> Have forfeited their ancient English dower
> Of inward happiness. We are selfish men.

In 1920 and in the succeeding years we as a nation not
only plumbed the depths of material selfishness, but we
were unbelievably blind. We were blind to what constituted our own enlightened self-interest, and we therefore
refused to see that by undertaking a measure of responsibility in maintaining world order, with the immediate
commitments which that might involve, we were insur-
ing our people and our democratic ideals against the perils of an unforeseeable future and we were safeguarding
our children and our children's children against having
to incur the same sacrifices as those forced upon their
fathers. Who can today compare the cost in life or treas-
ure which we might have had to contribute towards the
stabilization of a world order during its formative years
after 1919 with the prospective loss in lives and the lowering of living standards which will result from the supreme
struggle in which we are now engaged?

During the first century of our independence our forefathers were occupying and developing a continent. The

American pioneer was pushing ever westward across the Alleghenies into the fertile Ohio valley, the Mississippi and Missouri country, the Southwest, and finally to the Pacific Coast. The shock of disaster elsewhere in the world was hardly felt; relief from recurring depressions could always be found by expanding our frontiers, by opening up new lands and new industries to supply the needs of our rapidly expanding population. Thus cushioned against the impact of events abroad, the American standard of living steadily improved and became the hope of down-trodden peoples of other lands.

Protected by two great oceans to the east and to the west, with no enemies to the north or to the south, our people in the nineteenth century were imbued with the belief that their safety lay in their isolation from the rest of the world.

But the oceans shrank with the development of maritime communications, and the security which we enjoyed by reason of our friendly neighbors vanished with the growth of aviation.

And even in our earlier days our industries became increasingly dependent upon raw materials imported from abroad; their products were sold increasingly in the markets of the Old World. Our urban industrial areas in the east became more and more dependent on our agricultural and mining areas in the west. All became increasingly dependent on world markets and world sources of supply.

With the close of the first World War the period of our isolation had ended. Neither from the standpoint of our physical security nor from the standpoint of our material well-being could we any more remain isolated. But, as if by their fiat they could turn back the tides of accomplished fact, our leaders and the great majority of our people in those post-war years deliberately returned to the provincial policies and standards of an earlier day, thinking that because these had served their purpose in the past they could do so again in a new and in a changed world.

And now we are engaged in the greatest war which mankind has known. We are reaping the bitter fruit of our own folly and of our own lack of vision. We are paying dearly as well for the lack of statesmanship and for the crass errors of omission and of commission, so tragically evidenced in the policies of those other nations which have had their full share of responsibility for the conduct of human affairs during the past generation.

What can we now do to rectify the mistakes of those past two decades?

The immediate answer is self-evident. We must utterly and finally crush the evil men, and the iniquitous systems which they have devised, that are today menacing our existence and that of free men and women throughout the earth. There can be no compromise. There can be no respite until the victory is won. We are faced by desperate and powerful antagonists. To win the fight requires every ounce of driving energy, every resource and initiative, every sacrifice and every instinct of devotion which each and every American citizen possesses. None of us can afford to think of ourselves, none of us can dare to do less than his full part in the common effort. Our liberty, our Christian faith, our life as a free people, are at stake. Those who indulge themselves in false optimism, those who believe that the peoples who are fighting with us for our common cause should relieve us of our due share of sacrifice, those who are reluctant to give their all in this struggle for the survival on the earth of what is fine and decent, must be regarded as enemies of the American people.

Now more than ever before must we keep the faith with those who lie sleeping in this hallowed ground—and with those who now at this very hour are dying for the cause and for the land they love.

And after we win the victory—and we will—what then? Will the people of the United States then make certain that those who have died that we may live as free men and women shall not have died in vain?

I believe that in such case the voice of those who are doing the fighting, and the voice of those who are producing the arms with which we fight, must be heard and must be heeded.

And I believe that these voices of the men who will make our victory possible will demand that justice be done, inexorably and swiftly, to those individuals, groups, or peoples, as the case may be, that can truly be held accountable for the stupendous catastrophe into which they have plunged the human race. But I believe they will likewise wish to make certain that no element in any nation shall be forced to atone vicariously for crimes for which it is not responsible and that no people shall be forced to look forward to endless years of want and of starvation.

I believe they will require that the victorious nations joined with the United States undertake forthwith during the period of the armistice the disarmament of all nations, as set forth in the Atlantic Charter, which "may threaten aggression outside of their frontiers."

I believe they will insist that the United Nations undertake the maintenance of an international police power in the years after the war to insure freedom from fear to peace-loving peoples until there is established that permanent system of general security promised by the Atlantic Charter.

Finally I believe they will demand that the United Nations become the nucleus of a world organization of the future to determine the final terms of a just, an honest, and a durable peace to be entered into after the passing of the period of social and economic chaos which will come inevitably upon the termination of the present war and after the completion of the initial and gigantic task of relief, of reconstruction, and of rehabilitation which will confront the United Nations at the time of the armistice.

This is in very truth a people's war. It is a war which cannot be regarded as won until the fundamental rights of the peoples of the earth are secured. In no other manner can a true peace be achieved.

In the pre-war world large numbers of people were unemployed; the living standards of millions of people were pitifully low; it was a world in which nations were classified as "haves" and "have nots," with all that these words imply in terms of inequity and hatred.

The pre-war world was one in which small vociferous and privileged minorities in each country felt that they could not gain sufficient profits if they faced competition

from abroad. Even this country with its rich natural resources, its vast economic strength, a population whose
genius for efficient production enabled us to export the
finest products in the world at low cost and at the same
time to maintain the highest wages—a country whose
competitive strength was felt in the markets of the world
—even such a nation was long dominated by its minority
interests who sought to destroy international trade in
order to avoid facing foreign competition.

They not only sought to do so, but for long years following the first World War largely succeeded in doing so.
The destruction of international trade by special minority interests in this and in other countries brought ruin to
their fellow citizens by destroying an essential element
upon which the national prosperity in each country in
large measure depended. It helped to pave the way,
through the impoverishment and distress of the people,
for militarism and dictatorship. Can the democracies of
the world again afford to permit national policies to be
dictated by self-seeking minorities of special privilege?

The problem which will confront us when the years of
the post-war period are reached is not primarily one of
production. For the world can readily produce what mankind requires. The problem is rather one of distribution
and purchasing power: of providing the mechanism
whereby what the world produces may be fairly distrib-
uted among the nations of the world and of providing the
means whereby the people of the world may obtain the
world's goods and services. Your Government has already taken steps to obtain the support and active cooperation of others of the United Nations in this great task,

a task which in every sense of the term is a new frontier
. . . a frontier of limitless expanse . . . the frontier of
human welfare.

When the war ends, with the resultant exhaustion
which will then beset so many of the nations who are
joined with us, only the United States will have the
strength and the resources to lead the world out of the
slough in which it has struggled so long, to lead the way
toward a world order in which there can be freedom from
want. In seeking this end we will of course respect the
right of all peoples to determine for themselves the type
of internal economic organization which is best suited to
their circumstances. But I believe that here in our own
country we will continue to find the best expression for
our own and the general good under a system which will
give the greatest incentive and opportunity for individual enterprise. It is in such an environment that our citizens have made this country strong and great. Given
sound national policies directed toward the benefit of the
majority and not of the minority, and real security and
equality of opportunity for all, reliance on the ingenuity,
initiative, and enterprise of our citizens rather than on
any form of bureaucratic management will in the future
best assure the liberties and promote the material welfare
of our people.

In taking thought of our future opportunities we surely
must undertake to preserve the advantages we have
gained in the past. I cannot believe the peoples of the
United States and of the Western Hemisphere will ever
relinquish the inter-American system they have built up.
Based as it is on sovereign equality, on liberty, on peace,
and on joint resistance to aggression, it constitutes the

only example in the world today of a regional federation of free and independent peoples. It lightens the darkness of our anarchic world. It should constitute a cornerstone in the world structure of the future.

If this war is in fact a war for the liberation of peoples, it must assure the sovereign equality of peoples throughout the world, as well as in the world of the Americas. Our victory must bring in its train the liberation of all peoples. Discrimination between peoples because of their race, creed, or color must be abolished. The age of imperialism is ended. The right of a people to their freedom must be recognized, as the civilized world long since recognized the right of an individual to his personal freedom. The principles of the Atlantic Charter must be guaranteed to the world as a whole—in all oceans and in all continents.

And so, in the fulness of God's time when the victory is won, the people of the United States will once more be afforded the opportunity to play their part in the determination of the kind of world in which they will live. With courage and with vision they can yet secure the future safety of their country and of its free institutions and help the nations of the earth back into the paths of peace.

Then, on some future Memorial Day, the American people, as they mark the graves of those who died in battle for their country in these last two World Wars, can at last truly say: "Sleep on in quiet and in peace; the victory you made it possible for us to win has now been placed at the service of your country and of humanity; your sacrifice has not been made in vain."

Twenty-eight Nations
Joined for Liberty

A FEW of us here tonight were privileged to be present in the White House last Sunday at an historic
ceremony. That ceremony marked the adherence to the
Declaration of the United Nations of two new members
of the roll of honor.

It signalized the entrance into the rights and obligations of that pact of the people of the Commonwealth of
the Philippines whose epic resistance against the invad-
ing hordes, whose loyalty to their American brothers, will
never be forgotten by the people of the United States. No
nation has ever more fully earned its right to its independence.

That ceremony of last Sunday likewise marked the for-
mal adherence to the United Nations' Declaration of our
great neighbor the Republic of Mexico. In the annals of
our Western Hemisphere no nation has been more jealous
of her sovereign rights, more determined to preserve her
liberties, more staunch in upholding the principles of
inter-American solidarity upon which the security of the
New World depends, than Mexico. From the very outset
of the curse of Hitlerism the Government and people of
Mexico have seen the world issues clearly. They have, as
always, placed themselves squarely beneath the standard

of liberty. When, finally, the assassins of the seas slaughtered Mexican seamen engaged in legitimate and peaceful trade, Mexico in her proud tradition unhesitatingly
declared war upon the Axis powers. On June 14 the people
of Mexico became one of the United Nations.

Twenty-eight peoples—in all continents, of all creeds,
of all races—are now joined together in this highest of all
enterprises: the preservation of human liberty.

I think that all of us last Sunday felt equally that that
assembly of representatives of these twenty-eight united
nations, headed by the President of the United States,
symbolized two great assurances, the assurance that
through our unity the victory will unquestionably be
ours and the assurance that because of this very unity
we can look forward with hope and renewed faith to the
future after the war is won.

For cooperation between us all in this peoples' struggle
finally to destroy the curse of Hitlerism and the pestilence
of Japanese militarism is essential to the winning of this
war.

This lesson of the need for such cooperation has been a
hard-earned lesson. It was learned by some countries too
late to save them. It was learned by others on the very
brink of disaster. Some nations may not yet have learned
it. But it has been learned by the United Nations—and
the United Nations will win the war in consequence of it.

Will the tragic experiences which humanity underwent
between November, 1918, and September, 1939, also bear
fruit? Have we all learned in this hard and perilous way
that cooperation is no less essential in maintaining peace
than in winning a war?

During this war the people of the United Nations will

[77]

have lived in the constant shadow of danger. They will have offered their all to safeguard their liberties and to defend that which they hold dear.

When the war ends, these present shadows will lift; the immediate physical dangers will have passed.

The memory of man is sometimes short. We can none of us again afford to forget the lessons we have learned, that cooperation to win the victory is not enough, that there must be even greater cooperation to win the peace, if the peace is to be that kind of a peace which alone can prevent the recurrence of war—a peace which is more than a mere interlude between battles.

Without such cooperation we shall have again economic distress, unemployment, poverty, and suffering for millions of people—suffering which, while less acute, is longer drawn out and is but little less hard to bear than the miseries of war, suffering which, as surely as night follows day, is the breeder of wars.

In our conduct of the war we are all of us cooperating with confidence in each other, fully, completely. This form of partnership must obtain a momentum that will carry over into the post-war period. We must cultivate the habit.

The final terms of the peace should wait until the immediate tasks of the transition period after the defeat of the Axis powers have been completed by the United Nations and until the final judgments can be coolly and rationally rendered. But the organization through which the United Nations are to carry on their cooperation should surely be formed so far as practicable before the fires of war which are welding them together have cooled. Everything which can be done to this end before the war is over must be done. Every act or measure of cooperation among the United Nations must be scrutinized to see whether it cannot also be made to serve in the winning of the peace.

On June 11 last this Government concluded a master lend-lease agreement with the Soviet Union which deals with the principles of mutual aid in the conduct of the war. In this agreement the United States and the Soviet Union undertake to continue to furnish each other with supplies, information, and services needed for the war effort to the full extent of their ability. The agreement thus deals with a matter of prime importance from the standpoint of the war effort.

But this agreement also looks forward to the peace. The agreement reaffirms adherence to the Atlantic Charter, and the two Governments pledge themselves to cooperate with each other and all other nations of like mind in a concerted and determined effort to promote the betterment of world-wide economic relations.

Article VII of the agreement envisages international and domestic measures directed to the expansion of production, employment, and the exchange and consumption of goods, which are the material foundations of the liberty and welfare of all peoples. The best means of attaining these and other objectives, such as the elimination of all forms of discriminatory treatment in international commerce and the reduction of tariffs and other trade barriers, will be the subject of continuing conversations between the two Governments.

Similar master lend-lease agreements have thus far been concluded with three other countries in addition to the Soviet Union, with Great Britain on February 23,

1942, with the Republic of China on June 2, 1942, and yesterday with Belgium. Thus in effect five of the world's great nations have become partners, with full equality of status, in a new world understanding . . . an economic understanding, open to the participation of all other nations of like mind . . . an economic understanding which may well become the nucleus of a United Nations organization for the relief and economic reconstruction of the post-war world.

During the difficult transition period between the end of the war and the final conclusion of peace, there will be vital need for such an organization. Millions of the world's peoples will be homeless. In Europe and in Asia transportation systems will be ruined, production facilities destroyed, farms laid waste, cities devastated. We shall all of us be confronted with the gigantic task of converting to peacetime uses whole industries now producing munitions of war. There must be agreement upon the objectives to be attained, machinery for carrying out the agreed action of the United Nations, and cooperative effort of the highest order among all of the United Nations to which the oppressed peoples of the earth may look with hope when they have cast off their chains.

In these, our purposes and our endeavors, we in the United States are fortified by the knowledge that we may count upon the firm support and assistance of those of our neighbors of the New World who are not represented among the United Nations, but who have severed all relations with the Axis powers and who have thus refused to permit their territory to be utilized by agents of the tyrannies that have dared to attack the New World, against their fellow Americans, and against their own security. Eleven of the American Republics are now numbered among the United Nations. And in the supreme task of guarding the independence of the Western Hemisphere so that the liberties of all of the peoples of the Americas may be secure, we may well pay tribute tonight to the help and the encouragement which those of us engaged in war derive from all of the many practical and generous forms of support offered us by the Governments and people of Brazil, of Colombia and Venezuela, of Peru and Ecuador, of Bolivia, Paraguay, and Uruguay.

Throughout these past weeks the Axis submarines, when they have been able to do so, have already attacked and sunk indiscriminately merchant vessels of all the American nations. If they have adhered to any standards, such standards would have disgraced the pirates of the dark ages. Now the Hitlerite Government, by means of the announcement of a paper blockade, openly threatens to sink any vessel engaged in legitimate and lawful trade between the Eastern Coast of the United States and the rest of the hemisphere.

The American Republics have at all times insisted upon their untrammeled right to maintain inviolate freedom of communication between them. Their well-being, their very existence, depends upon the exercise of this right. I cannot believe that any of the free peoples of the Americas will ever acquiesce in the brazen effort of Hitlerite Germany to cow them into accepting Hitler's dictation as to the manner in which they shall enjoy their rights as members of the American family of nations.

As we meet here tonight men and women in all parts of the world are dying for the sake of the cause which we uphold. The Chetnik in the mountains of Yugoslavia, the guerrillas in Greece, the patriots of Czechoslovakia, Poland, Norway, Holland, Belgium, Luxemburg—yes, and of occupied France—who are murdered daily by the agents of the Gestapo, are all of them offering up their lives because of their belief in what you and I believe.

The valiant armies of the Chinese who have successfully withstood the Japanese onslaught for five cruel years; the superb hosts of the Soviet Union whose matchless resistance long since turned the tide; the fighting men of Canada, of Australia, of New Zealand, of South Africa; of the British Navy, of the British Army, and of the British Air Force, who have for so long borne the burden and heat of the struggle; and now of our own Navy, of our own Army, and of our own Air Force, are all of them fighting gallantly—and, thank God, successfully—joined in one common objective: the great objective to preserve our common liberties and to make men free.

Through the union of the United Nations their victory will be assured.

In the words which the President spoke last Sunday, "Man, born to freedom in the image of God, will not forever suffer the oppressors' sword. The peoples of the United Nations are taking that sword from the oppressors' hands."

Free Access to Raw Materials

JUST a year has passed since I last had the privilege of addressing the National Foreign Trade Convention. During the short space of these twelve months the people of the United States have passed through some of the most portentous events they have known in their entire history. They have experienced the most far-reaching changes in their national life which they have yet undergone. They are confronting the gravest dangers they have ever yet had to face. They are now engaged in the greatest war that mankind has suffered.

And yet as we look back over the record of these past twelve months, I think we may well feel proud that we are American citizens. From the moment of the attack upon Pearl Harbor the people of the United States have rallied magnificently.

Owing to the nature of the universal war in which we were plunged, it became immediately necessary to send our troops to far-flung outposts in the seven seas. The gigantic difficulties in the carrying-out of the strategic plans involved stagger the imagination. They have been met successfully. We are raising the greatest army our people have ever needed, and we all of us know the superb way in which that task has been carried out. Every day that passes our Navy justifies more completely the historic pride which the American people have held in it.

And in the field of production the vast goals announced by the President last winter will in some particulars not only be met, but be surpassed. Our production will be far greater than any but a very few of our citizens could then have expected.

At this very moment, our Air Force, our Army, and our Navy are fighting with our allies in regions of the Atlantic and of the North Pacific, in many parts of Asia and of the South Pacific, in the Mediterranean and the Near East, and are likewise joined with our neighbors of the Americas in guarding the Western Hemisphere. Every hour that passes, these forces of ours are becoming stronger and more efficient. Nor do we ever forget the memory of those who, in the defense of our liberties, have already gallantly laid down their lives in battle against our enemies.

None of us can deny that some of us have fallen down on our jobs: nor that some of us have not realized fully enough the stark evil of the foes who confront us, the vastness of the military resources of our enemies, nor the magnitude of the stupendous task which lies ahead of us. Many of us do not yet realize fully how great are the sacrifices every citizen must make to insure the success of the war effort, nor the inescapable fact that the individual life of every one of us is going to be changed as a result of the holocaust in which the world has been plunged by the criminals of the Axis powers.

But I have never thought that the American people

needed to be browbeaten or bludgeoned into defending their independence and their homes. What the American people require is to be told the truth, as the President of the United States, with courage, with foresight, and with utter frankness, has been telling it to them. They can take it. And when they know the facts, no people on earth are capable of greater accomplishment.

Democracies may take long to prepare for war or to engage in war, but when the free men and women of a democracy such as ours are at war to preserve their liberty and their faith, they will never fail to excel the regimented slaves of the dictators. We are fighting for our own independence and for the right to live in a decent and a peaceful world. The hosts of Hitler, of the Japanese war lords, and of the Italian Fascist racketeers are being slaughtered because of the insane delusion of their masters that they could make the resources of the world their own individual loot.

Of the outcome of this gigantic contest I have not the shadow of a doubt. For I am not one of those few who believe that "we are losing this war." I not only believe that we are going to win this war, but I know that however long the struggle may be, however mountainous the obstacles that must yet be overcome, the American people will never lay down their arms until the final and complete victory is won by the United Nations.

In the grim struggle which lies before us we are fighting side by side with the other partners of the United Nations.

Never in the long centuries of modern history have men and women fought more gloriously than have the armies of the Soviet Union. Their epic and successful resistance to the onslaughts of Hitler's forces a year ago not only gave the lie to Hitler's boasts that he could crush the Russian Army, but constituted in itself the major triumph of the United Nations in the war until that time. And once more through the long summer of 1942 the Soviet heroes have held firm.

We don't hear Hitler tell the German people this year that the Soviet Union will quickly crumble before his offensive. He doesn't dare. For he knows that the German people have learned to their bitter cost that Hitler's promises in this case, as they will soon learn they are in every case, are but the empty lies of a rapidly deflating demagogue.

The United States and its associates among the United Nations must render the utmost measure of assistance to the Soviet Union. Whether that assistance be through the furnishing of arms, equipment, or supplies or whether that assistance be by means of the diversion of German armies forced upon Hitler through the creation of a new theater of operations, the fullest measure of every means of help will be given. The surest way to insure the defeat of Hitler is to give this help and to give it unstintingly at the earliest possible moment.

The amazing efforts of the British Air Force in its all-out attacks upon Germany have long since shown the German people how much value they can attach to the assurances given them by the Nazi leaders that Germany would never be bombed. The havoc and devastation created by these British flyers, now joined by our own Air Forces, are crippling war plants, munitions factories, shipyards, and railways and gravely impairing the German effort to maintain the earlier levels of war production.

Nor can we here in the United States ever fail to remember with profound gratitude and renewed encouragement that eleven of the other Republics of the Americas are joined with us side by side in the war, and that seven other Republics have severed all relations with the Axis and are rendering their neighbors who are at war every form of cooperation and assistance. It is true that the remaining two Republics of the twenty-one have still refrained from carrying out the unanimous recommendations of the Inter-American Conference of Rio de Janeiro, in which they themselves joined, that all of the Americas sever all relations with the Axis, and are still permitting their territory to be utilized by the officials and the subversive agents of the Axis as a base for hostile activities against their neighbors. As a result of the reports on Allied ship movements sent by these agents, Brazilian, Cuban, Mexican, Colombian, Dominican, Uruguayan, Argentine, Chilean, Panamanian, and United States ships have been sunk without warning while plying between the American Republics, and as a result many nationals of these countries have lost their lives within the waters of the Western Hemisphere. But I cannot believe that these two Republics will continue long to permit their brothers and neighbors of the Americas, engaged as they are in a life and death struggle to preserve the liberties and the integrity of the New World, to be stabbed in the back by Axis emissaries operating in the territory, and under the free institutions, of these two Republics of the Western Hemisphere.

Not until freedom was in mortal danger throughout the earth did liberty-loving nations fully learn the lesson of collaboration. Had that lesson been learned earlier, had the United Nations found their unity in anticipation of attack rather than under the urgent pressure of attack, the maximum effectiveness of our war effort would have been reached far more speedily. It is now evident that in the cooperation and unity of the United Nations lies our ultimate victory. I believe that it is equally true that in the continuance and timeliness of that cooperation also lies our hope for an honest, a workable, and a lasting peace.

The unity which the free peoples have achieved to win their war must continue on to win their peace. For since this is in truth a people's war, it must be followed by a people's peace. The translation into terms of reality of the promise of the great freedoms for all people everywhere is the final objective. We must be beforehand in charting the course toward that objective. The clearer we can make the outlines of the peace, the firmer will be our determination to attain it, the stronger our will to win the war.

One hears it said that no thought should be given to the problems of the peace, nor to the problems of the transitional period between war and established peace, until after the war has been won. The shallowness of such thinking, whether sincere or sinister, is apparent. In many cases it is due, I think, to what Plato terms "double ignorance": when a man is ignorant that he is ignorant.

It does not detract from our war effort, nor from the single-minded drive of the nation towards the ultimate victory, that our people should be thinking of and planning for the kind of world of the future in which peace can be maintained and in which men and women can live out their lives in security and free from fear. Such efforts in my judgment contribute directly to the drive towards victory.

The setting-up now of efficient machinery to deal with such problems as relief and rehabilitation, for example, which will accompany victory, cannot fail to strengthen the resolve of all liberty-loving peoples, including those in areas now occupied by the enemy, to bring the conflict to the speediest possible conclusion. It cannot fail to make them realize that the sort of world for which we are striving is worth the sacrifices of war, is worth the cost of victory.

It is clear to all of us, I think, that the United Nations must maintain their unity beyond the immediate task of prosecuting the people's war in order to prepare for and insure to the people their peace.

Point Four of the Atlantic Charter promises "to further the enjoyment by all States, great or small, victor or vanquished, of access, on equal terms, to the trade and to the raw materials of the world which are needed for their economic prosperity."

This promise, and the balance of the Charter, the United Nations adopted as their own by their common declaration of last January 1.

How do they propose to make it real?

Some things at least are clear.

Access to raw materials does not mean and cannot mean that every nation, or any nation, can have the source of all of them within its borders. That is not the way the world was put together. Coal and iron in combination are found in few locations. Much of the nickel of the world is in one great Canadian deposit. Neither coffee nor cinchona will grow in the United States. No nation can be self-sufficient by changes in its boundaries, and those who try by force to do so, as the Axis leaders have tried, bring on themselves inevitably only their own destruction. The path to plentiful supplies does not lie through physical control of the sources of supply.

The problem of raw materials is not exclusively, or even primarily, a problem of colonial or undeveloped areas. The great mineral deposits exist chiefly in countries that are already self-governing, such as the United States, the Soviet Union, Canada, Germany, Sweden, South Africa, Mexico, Brazil. Access to raw materials does not mean possession of a colony. It means effective power to buy in the world's markets.

The legal right to export raw materials has seldom been restricted by producing countries. True, the United States and other countries sometimes have been guilty of forbidding the export of certain things needed for production elsewhere, for fear that others might obtain the means to trespass on their markets. But those cases were rare. Countries producing raw materials desired normally to sell their surplus, and the problem usually was to find a profitable market. The right to buy was real, and satisfied peace-loving peoples. Belgium, Denmark, Sweden, Switzerland, Czechoslovakia, Norway, not to speak of the United States and England, bought in the years between the wars great quantities of foreign raw materials, and none of them claimed that they needed greater resources to live. The countries that complained, and shrieked that they must have colonies or die, have shown now by their conduct that what they wanted was not prosperity and peace, but the materials for making war.

For war, indeed, one cannot count on overseas supplies, and an aggressor must first corner all he can of coal and iron and oil and copper, in the ground or out of it.

But the Atlantic Charter does not propose to aid aggression. It proposes, on the contrary, to make sure that aggression does not happen, and to that end the United Nations will create the necessary instruments—and this time they will be effective instruments and must be firmly used—to make it certain that any power that again threatens to enslave its neighbors is denied the means to do so. The materials of war must be denied to any future Hitler.

The access to raw materials of which the Charter speaks is access for the purposes of peace. For that purpose it matters little in whose territory particular resources are found. Access means the right to buy in peaceful trade, and it exists whenever that right is effective and secure.

What forces, then, have interfered with that right in the past or may interfere with it in the future?

Most raw materials are not subject to monopolistic practices because producers are too numerous; but there have been charges in the past, and there are charges now, that in certain cases the producers of some commodities with the support of the governments to which they owed allegiance have managed, by what our Sherman Law calls combinations in restraint of trade, to reduce supplies and enhance prices beyond reasonable levels or to discriminate among their customers. A world devoted to increased production and fair and fruitful exchange of all kinds of useful goods cannot tolerate such practices.

But monopoly in the field of raw materials is not the major problem. Most materials are plentiful in peace, and their producers want to sell them to any customer who has the means to buy. The real problem of consumers has always been the means of payment. In the world that emerges from the war that problem will be very serious indeed.

When this war ends, much of the world will be impoverished beyond anything known in modern times.

Relief cannot go on forever, and the day must come as soon as possible when the devastated areas again are self-supporting. That will require enormous shipments from abroad, both of capital goods and of the raw materials of industry. For these early reconstruction shipments no immediate means of payment will be visible. That means large financing, much of it long-term. The United Nations must arrange that too. But finally comes payment, both of whatever interest burden the loans carry and for the current purchases of raw materials and other imports. I need not tell this audience that international payments, on that scale, can be made only in goods and services. There is no other way. Access to raw materials comes in the end to access to the great buying markets of the world. Those who expect to export must take the world's goods and services in payment. I hope that the United States is ready now to act upon that lesson.

The United Nations have agreed to act upon it, and in mutual-aid agreements with a growing number of them we and they have promised to direct our common efforts to increased production, employment, and the exchange and consumption of all kinds of useful goods. We and they have promised further to attack the problem by removing discriminations in the treatment of international trade and by reducing unwarranted and artificial tariff barriers. The future prosperity and peace of the world and of the United States depend vitally on the good faith and the thoroughness with which we and they together carry out those promises.

During the war as fully as we can, and more fully after we have destroyed the madmen who seek to rule the world by force and terror, we of the United Nations will go forward in a loyal partnership to carry out the pledges we have made to each other and the world.

There is no limit, then, to the material prosperity which is within the reach of the United States and of mankind. The great thing that has happened in our time is that mankind at long last has taught itself enough of the means and techniques of production, of transport, and of scientific agriculture so that it is technically possible to produce and to distribute on this planet the basic physical necessities of health and decent living for all of the world's people. What remains, and it is a great and formidable task, is so to remake our relations with each other, in loyal and cooperative effort, that the great productive forces which are within our sight may function freely for the benefit of all. It is within our power to make a mighty start upon that road; we have laid down the principles of action; it is for the people of the United States to determine whether their Government is to be authorized to carry on.

For twelve tragic years after the close of the last World

War the United States withdrew from almost every form of constructive cooperation with the other nations of the earth. We are reaping the bitter cost of that isolation.

For I am persuaded that after the victory is won, so long as the power and influence of the United States are felt in the councils of the world, so long as our cooperation is effectively offered, so long can one hope that peace can and will be maintained.

The blessings we have inherited from our forefathers do not constitute an inheritance that we may only passively enjoy. They can only be preserved by sacrifice, by courage, by resolution, and by vision. If the American people prove themselves worthy of their ancestors, if they still possess their forefathers' dauntless courage and their ability to meet new conditions with wisdom and determination, the future of this nation will rest secure, and our children and our children's children will be able to live out their lives in safety and in peace.

Blueprint for Peace

TONIGHT we of the United Nations have the right
to look ahead, not only with hope and with passion-
ate conviction, but with the assurance which high military achievement affords, to the ultimate victory which
will presage a Free World.

None of us are so optimistic as to delude ourselves into
the belief that the end is in sight or that we have not still
before us grave obstacles, dark days, reverses and great
sacrifices yet to be undergone. But the tremendous initial effort, in the case of our own country, of transforming
the inertia of a democracy of 130 millions of people at
peace into the driving, irresistible energy of 130 millions
of American citizens aroused and united in war, has been
successfully made.

The first months of confusion and of cross-currents are
past. The men and women of the United States are now
enabled to see for themselves the development of the
strategic moves in which their Commander-in-Chief and
their military and naval leaders are engaged. They are
able to appreciate the amazing nature of the feat realized
in the occupation of North Africa and to recognize the
time and the extent of the preparation required for this
gigantic task.

They now realize that the prodding of our self-ap-
pointed pundits who were constantly demanding the

creation of a second front was not required and that the carefully thought-out plans for the second front now in being had long since been conceived and were already in process of realization while the clamor of these critics went on.

They can now fully evaluate the lack of vision and of knowledge of those who demanded the abandonment of our whole policy towards the French people, at the very moment that that policy was afforded the striking opportunity of proving its full worth—its full worth to the cause for which we fight and its full worth in preserving the soul of France during the darkest days she has ever known: France, the birthplace of so many of those principles of human liberty for which we and the people of France once more battle today.

They realize that we have in North Africa but one objective, the defeat of the Axis forces, which will bring with it the liberation of the people of France. During these first days all arrangements which we may make with Frenchmen in North Africa are solely military in character and are undertaken—properly—by the American and British military commanders. It is the hope of all of us that all Frenchmen who represent or who are part of the forces of resistance to Hitler will unite as one in the support of our military endeavor.

And so the clouds are lifting—the clouds of doubt and of disparagement and of lack of self-confidence. We can all see more clearly how inevitable has now become the final conquest of the armies of that criminal paranoiac whom the German people were so benighted as to acclaim as their leader, how crushing will at long last be the defeat which the Japanese hordes and their military leaders will suffer in just retribution for the treacherous barbarity which they have been inflicting upon the world during the past eleven years.

How can we achieve that Free World, the attainment of which alone can compensate mankind for the stupendous sacrifices which human beings everywhere are now being called upon to suffer?

Our military victory will only be won, in Churchill's immortal words, by blood and tears, and toil and sweat.

It is just as clear that the Free World which we must achieve can only be attained, not through the expenditure of toil and sweat alone but also through the exercise of all of the wisdom which men of today have gained from the experience of the past, and by the utilization not only of idealism but also of the practical knowledge of the working of human nature and of the laws of economics and of finance.

What the United Nations' blueprint imperatively requires is to be drafted in the light of experience and of common sense and in a spirit of justice, of democracy, and of tolerance, by men who have their eyes on the stars, but their feet on the ground. In the fundamentals of international relationships there is nothing more fatally dangerous than the common American fallacy that the formulation of an aspiration is equivalent to the hard-won realization of an objective. Of this basic truth we have no more tragic proof than the Kellogg-Briand Pact.

It seems to me that the first essential is the continuous and rapid perfecting of a relationship between the United Nations so that this military relationship may be further strengthened by the removal of all semblance of disunity or of suspicious rivalry and by the clarification of the

Free World goals for which we are fighting, and so that the form of international organization determined to be best suited to achieve international security will have developed to such an extent that it can fully operate as soon as the present military partnership has achieved its purpose of complete victory.

Another essential is the reaching of agreements between the United Nations before the armistice is signed upon those international adjustments, based upon the universal principles of the Atlantic Charter and pursuant to the pledges contained in our mutual-aid agreements with many of our allies, which we believe to be desirable and necessary for the maintenance of a peaceful and prosperous world of the future.

We all envisage the tragic chaos and anarchy which will have engulfed Europe and a great part of the rest of the world by the time Hitler's brief day is done, and when he and his accomplices confront their judges. The United Nations' machinery for relief and rehabilitation must be prepared to operate without a moment's delay to alleviate the suffering and misery of millions of homeless and starving human beings, if civilization is to be saved from years of social and moral collapse.

"No one will go hungry or without the other means of livelihood in any territory occupied by the United Nations, if it is humanly within our powers to make the necessary supplies available to them. Weapons will also be supplied to the peoples of these territories to hasten the defeat of the Axis." This is the direction of the President to the Lend-Lease Administrator, to General Eisenhower, and to the Department of State, and it is being carried out by them to the full extent of their power and resources. The other United Nations, each to the full extent of its ability, will, I am sure, cooperate whole-heartedly in this great task.

Through prearrangement certain measures such as the disarmament of aggressor nations laid down in the Atlantic Charter must likewise be undertaken rapidly and with the utmost precision.

Surely we should not again resort to the procedures adopted in 1919 for the settlement of the future of the world. We cannot afford to permit the basic issues by which the destiny of humanity will be determined to be resolved without prior agreement, in hurried confusion, by a group of harassed statesmen working against time, pressed from one side by the popular demand for immediate demobilization and crowded on the other by the exigencies of domestic politics.

If we are to attain our Free World—the world of the Four Freedoms—to the extent practicable, the essential principles of international political and economic relations in that new world must be agreed upon in advance and with the full support of each one of the United Nations, so that agreements to be reached will implement those principles.

If the people of the United States now believe as a result of the experience of the past twenty-five years that the security of our Republic is vitally affected by the fate of the other peoples of the earth, they will recognize that the nature of the international political and economic relations which will obtain in the world after victory has been achieved is to us a matter of profound self-interest.

As the months pass, two extreme schools of thought will become more and more vocal—the first, stemming from the leaders of the group which preached extreme isolation, will once more proclaim that war in the rest of the world every twenty years or so is inevitable, that we can stay out if we so desire, and that any assumption by this country of any form of responsibility for what goes on in the world means our unnecessary involvement in war; the other, of which very often men of the highest idealism and sincerity are the spokesmen, will maintain that the United States must assume the burdens of the entire globe, must see to it that the standards in which we ourselves believe must immediately be adopted by all of the peoples of the earth, and must undertake to inculcate in all parts of the world our own policies of social and political reform whether the other peoples involved so desire or not. While under a different guise, this school of thought is in no way dissimilar in theory from the strange doctrine of incipient "bear the white man's burden" imperialism which flared in this country in the first years of this century.

The people of the United States today realize that the adoption of either one of these two philosophies would prove equally dangerous to the future well-being of our nation.

Our Free World must be founded on the Four Freedoms: freedom *of* speech and *of* religion and freedom *from* want and *from* fear.

I do not believe that the two first freedoms—of speech and of religion—can ever be assured to mankind so long as want and war are permitted to ravage the earth. Freedom of speech and of religion need only protection; they require only relief from obstruction.

Freedom from fear—the assurance of peace—and freedom from want—the assurance of individual personal security—require all of the implementation which the genius of man can devise through effective forms of international cooperation.

Peace—freedom from fear—cannot be assured until the nations of the world, particularly the great powers, and that includes the United States, recognize that the threat of war anywhere throughout the globe threatens their own security and until they are jointly willing to exercise the police powers necessary to prevent such threats from materializing into armed hostilities.

And since policemen might be tyrants if they had no political superiors, freedom from fear also demands some form of organized international political cooperation to make the rules of international living and to change them as the years go by, and some sort of international court to adjudicate disputes. With effective institutions of that character to insure equity and justice, and the continued will to make them work, the peoples of the world should at length be able to live out their lives in peace.

Freedom from want requires these things: People who want to work must be able to find useful jobs, not sometimes, not in good years only, but continuously. These jobs must be at things which they do well and which can be done well in the places where they work. They must be able to exchange the things which they produce, on fair terms, for other things which other people, often in other places, can make better than they.

Efficient and continuous production and fair exchange are both necessary to the abundance which we seek, and they depend upon each other. In the past we have succeeded better with production than exchange. Production is called into existence by the prospects of exchange, prospects which have constantly been thwarted by all kinds of inequalities, imperfections, and restrictions. The problem of removing obstacles to fair exchange—the problem of distribution of goods and purchasing power —is far more difficult than the problem of production.

It will take much wisdom, much cooperative effort, and much surrender of private, short-sighted, and sectional self-interest to make these things all come true. But the goal is freedom from want—individual security and national prosperity—and is everlastingly worth striving for.

As mankind progresses on the path towards the goal of freedom from want and from fear, freedom of religion and of speech will more and more become a living reality. Never before have peace and individual security been classed as freedom. Never before have they been placed alongside of religious liberty and free speech as human freedoms which should be inalienable. Upon these Four Freedoms must rest the structure of the future Free World.

This time there must be no compromise between justice and injustice, no yielding to expediency, no swerving from the great human rights and liberties established by the Atlantic Charter itself.

In the words of our President: "We shall win this war, and in Victory, we shall seek not vengeance, but the establishment of an international order in which the spirit of Christ shall rule the hearts of men and of nations."

We won't get a Free World any other way.

Dedication to
the Future

W E ARE MEETING this evening in St. Paul's
Church at Eastchester, New York, to pay tribute
to the memory of Sara Delano Roosevelt, the great
mother of a great son.

By the erection of this memorial to Mrs. Roosevelt,
generations still to come will remember that it was
largely due to her devoted interest and assistance that
there was made possible the restoration of this historic
church—the Shrine to the Bill of Rights—a sanctuary
that has always since 1733 been identified in the minds
of the people of the United States with that great right
later established in our Constitution: the freedom of
the press.

For nine years Mrs. Roosevelt was the chairman of
the restoration committee which at length succeeded in
the task of renewing this grand memorial of our colonial
days, so that it now stands once again in its original
beauty. To that task Mrs. Roosevelt gave of herself generously and untiringly as she did in so many countless
ways and for so many worthy causes throughout the
years of her life.

Mrs. Roosevelt was the life-long friend of some of us gathered here. And I think we feel her gracious presence very near to us as we meet in this old church that was so close to her heart. None of us who had the privilege of her friendship can ever fail to be grateful for it. For no more loyal, no more devoted and unselfish friend could any man or woman have. Her transparent integrity of soul and mind, her radiant goodness, her charm of personality, and above all else, perhaps, her love for her fellow men have engraved her image deep in the hearts of all of us. That image will not grow dim.

We are gathered together in these dedication ceremonies on the eve of the first anniversary of that treacherous attack upon the United States which involved our people in this great World War which has engulfed all of the continents of the earth.

It is a solemn moment as we think back over the crowded history of these past twelve months, during which our united people and their Government have made the supreme effort to preserve the freedom with which this land of ours has been blessed and to turn the tides of battle towards the ultimate victory of the great cause which we uphold—the cause of human liberty.

We think back to those first difficult months when we had to achieve the readjustment of our national life in all of its phases so as to insure an all-out war effort, and to the months thereafter when the long and difficult task of translating military and naval plans into accomplishment had to be realized. Now at the end of this twelve-month period, the strategy which our Government has been devising has become clear. The successes of our military and naval forces and of those of the peoples who are fighting at our side have instilled in us new hope and re-newed conviction. It may well be, however, that a dark and anxious time may yet have to be traversed before the ultimate victory, which we know we will attain, is won. Until that time, the efforts, the devotion, and the sacrifices of every one of us must be consecrated to the supreme task of winning the war.

But there are many of us today who are thinking back further than the anniversary of Pearl Harbor. They are thinking back over the past quarter of a century and are asking themselves whether this shattering world upheaval in which all of mankind is engaged was in fact inevitable.

They are asking themselves: If at the conclusion of the last World War the Government of the United States, in association with the other governments of free peoples, had sought the ideal which Woodrow Wilson once held up before the eyes of the people of this country—"a universal dominion of right by such a concert of free peoples as shall bring peace and safety to all nations and make the world itself at last free"—would this tragedy have come to pass?

The foreign policy of any nation must inevitably be a policy of self-interest. The foreign policy of the United States should ever be a policy based upon that course and upon those principles which, in the judgment of the American people themselves, will most clearly further the individual interest of their country and the general welfare of the people of the United States.

And I think a question that we can well afford to ask ourselves, on the eve of the anniversary of our entrance into the present war, is whether the policy pursued by the people of the United States during the years subsequent to the end of the last World War has proved in any sense to be to the interest or to the individual advantage of the American people. During that period we refused to assume the slightest measure of responsibility for the maintenance of world order. During the greater portion of that period we divorced ourselves from almost every form of cooperation with other powers, and as a people and as a government we stood aside while the forces which resulted in Hitlerism and all that which Hitlerism implies were shaping themselves. We stood aside pretending to ourselves that the United States could keep itself secure and free from danger even if all the rest of the world went up in flames.

From the standpoint of narrow and selfish self-interest alone, there are two straight questions which we might well ask ourselves. The cost of our participation in the war and of our military and naval production will burden the United States with a staggering national debt which must be paid by the taxpayers of this country. To win this struggle we are necessarily diverting the greater portion of our tremendous productive capacity into channels of destruction, not those of construction, and the debt burden which will have been created will inevitably affect the manner of life of every one of us and will inevitably diminish the opportunity for the progressive advancement of the generation to come.

Would we not as a people have been better advised if we had been willing twenty years ago to join with the other free peoples of the earth in promoting an international order which would have maintained the peace of the world and which could have prevented the rise of those conditions which have resulted in the total war of today? Is it conceivable that the material sacrifices which we might have been called upon to undertake to maintain world order in those earlier years could have involved a thousandth part of the material sacrifices which we are called upon today to undertake?

And the second question we may well ask ourselves is a question which hits straight at every family in the United States which has a father, or a son, or a brother serving this country today in the armed forces of the United States. Had the American people been willing a generation ago to bear their fair share of responsibility for the maintenance of world order, would our men today be forced to offer up their lives in order that they may insure the preservation of the independence and the security of their fellow citizens?

Already we hear again the voices of those who decry all forms of practical international cooperation. Already we can see the efforts of those who would make this fundamental issue—the issue of our national future—a question of party politics. Already we can once more follow the machinations of those special-privilege interests which would again turn the policy of the United States into one of narrow isolation, because of their belief that they themselves would profit through such a course.

Surely this is a question which transcends the bounds of any aspect of party and any claim of material advantage by a special few.

Today we are fighting this war in the closest collaboration with the governments joined with us. Our military operations, so successfully carried out recently on different fronts, have required effective cooperation and understanding with our allies. The very conduct of the war makes it indispensable that this form of agreement as to the strategy of our military and naval undertakings be continued by all of the governments of the United Nations. Our own security depends upon it.

We realize now that in this war this form of association of free peoples, struggling to preserve their liberty, is vitally necessary for the safety of our nation.

Do we realize that an association of the free peoples of the United Nations when the war is won is just as essential to the future security of this country? Surely we must assure ourselves when we achieve the victory for which we are fighting that this free people of ours, joined with the other free peoples who are fighting at our side, will see to it that the necessary measures of international cooperation are undertaken so that this catastrophe will not occur again.

In this shrine dedicated to the freedoms which we, the American people, by an inalienable right enjoy, we may well dedicate ourselves to the supreme task of the creation in the future of a world in which all peoples may in truth be free—free from the fear of war and assured of the right to live out their lives in safety and in peace.

The Victory of Peace

I AM deeply conscious of the privilege you have afforded me of addressing this Convocation of the
University of Toronto. During the century of its magnificently vigorous life this great institution of learning
has become, in the field of education, one of the recognized glories of our New World. In its notable contribu-
tions to the welfare of humanity and to the inspiration
of the human spirit, all of us who are citizens of the
Western Hemisphere can justly feel satisfaction and
pride. It is for that reason that I am so greatly honored
by the degree which the University of Toronto is today
conferring upon me.

I know, of course, of the long line of graduates from
these halls who have distinguished themselves in so
many varied branches of public endeavor, and I am
therefore also peculiarly gratified that from now on I
may lay claim—at least an honorary claim—to a connection with the University from which graduated the
present Prime Minister of Canada.

You will, I feel, permit me to say that while I know
how highly and how justly his outstanding abilities and
achievements are recognized in other parts of the world,
there is no place outside his own country where he has
won more affectionate regard, or a higher measure of
sincere admiration, than in the United States. The peo-

ples of our two countries are singularly blessed, in these the most critical moments of their history, that the guidance of the destinies of our two nations should have . been entrusted at this time to two men, Mackenzie King and Franklin Roosevelt, who have ever believed in the need for complete confidence and understanding between the peoples of Canada and of the United States and who have done more than any other two men similarly placed in the course of our national lives to strengthen in real and practical fashion that friendship which is so vital to the well-being and to the security of us both.

Today our peoples are fighting side by side to defend their liberties and to bring to utter defeat the band of dictators who have dared to think they could extinguish the light of democracy in the modern world. And we recognize fully how long and bitter the road may still be before the final victory is won.

Canada and the United States have had very similar problems in this war. We have met them in similar ways, and in collaboration, in the spirit of the Ogdensburg and the Hyde Park agreements. Our naval and military forces are cooperating closely in both oceans and on our land frontiers. In production we have both faced shortages of raw materials, labor, and manufacturing facilities, and our Governments have imposed effective, and often parallel, controls to overcome these shortages. We have both put our civilian economy on rations, increased taxation, and regulated prices. We have sought to supply each other with the things of which one of us was short and to coordinate our production facilities and resources in the most effective ways.

Both of us are arsenals of the United Nations, and in that too we have followed a like policy. That policy is, first, that food and munitions are dispatched to the places where they can be most useful in the conduct of the common war; and, second, that deliveries to countries that are not in position to make payment now are on terms that do not create impossible financial obligations later. Both of us are seeking to avoid the creation of uncollectible and trouble-breeding war debts.

The present high degree of economic cooperation between our two countries for the purpose of making as great a contribution as possible to the pooled war effort of the United Nations is extremely gratifying to us and must be so to our allies. Fortunately, the groundwork for this close collaboration was laid years before the outbreak of war. I refer primarily to the two reciprocal trade agreements between us, the first of which entered into force on January 1, 1936, and the second of which, replacing the first, became effective on January 1, 1939, the first day of the year in which Hitler forced upon Europe the war that was destined to spread over the globe.

The trade agreements we entered into in the days of precarious peace went a long way to heal the economic wounds, and attendant ill feeling, each of us had dealt the other in earlier years after the first World War.

On my side of the line, there had been the so-called Emergency Tariff Act of 1921, followed immediately by a general upward revision of the tariff in the Act of 1922; then, on the brink of the worst economic depression the world has suffered, came the monumental barrier created by the Hawley-Smoot Tariff Act of 1930. In our

Revenue Act of 1932, two of the four products subjected to new excise taxes by means of a rider to that legislation—lumber and copper—were and are of great interest to Canada. These measures in their collective effect struck hard at the trade of other countries. Canada felt the effects as much as any other country—perhaps more than any other.

Action on your side of the line was not slow in coming. You may recall that Canadian duties on a considerable number of products normally imported from the United States were raised automatically to the levels provided for on the same products in our Tariff Act of 1930. Everyone remembers the Ottawa Agreements of 1932, when the members of the British Commonwealth of Nations turned their backs upon the United States and all countries and made a desperate effort to make up for lost and depressed markets elsewhere by tariff preferences intended to encourage an expansion of trade within the British Empire. Every country felt the effects of the Ottawa Agreements, none, I believe, more than did the United States.

I mention these historical facts because they serve to remind us of past mistakes, still by no means completely remedied, that must be avoided after this war, most costly of all in men and wealth, has been brought to an end by our common victory. They also serve to emphasize the fundamental necessity of carrying forward constructively the task of economic cooperation between us begun with the first trade agreement and continued ever since.

The Governments of your country and mine see eye

to eye on this. They have formally declared their intention to seek common goals in peace as well as in war.

On November 30 last, in an exchange of notes, our two Governments took another important step along the road to a better world after victory. We agreed not only to try to promote mutually advantageous economic relations between ourselves, but to seek the cooperation of other nations of like mind in promoting the betterment of world-wide economic relations. These aims involve appropriate national and international measures to expand production, employment, and the exchange and consumption of goods; elimination of all forms of discriminatory treatment in international commerce; reduction of tariffs and other trade barriers; and, generally, attainment of the economic objectives of the Atlantic Charter, through the collaboration of the United Nations which are willing to join with us in the realization of these objectives.

Many of the United Nations, through Article VII of their mutual-aid agreements with the United States, have already joined in this same declaration of post-war economic objectives.

Our two countries, in the same exchange of notes, have expressed our intention to do something concrete about our declaration of aims by discussing soon with other United Nations how we two and other like-minded nations can agree upon a program to carry out these aims. They seek to furnish to the world practical evidence of the ways in which two neighboring countries that have a long experience of friendly relations and a high degree of economic interdependence, and that share the conviction that such reciprocally beneficial relations must form part of a general system, may promote by agreed action their mutual interests to the benefit of themselves and other countries.

I am not so bold as to venture a prediction here as to the details of such a program. However, I am confident that we can march together with other forward-looking nations along the road to a fruitful and secure post-war world, provided the people on both sides of the line support their Governments with understanding and determination in their efforts to do everything within their power to achieve these great objectives.

When the war ends, similar problems will face us both. We shall both confront the task of demobilization, and we shall both endeavor to make sure that the young men—and the young women—who are discharged from military service have a real chance to find useful and productive employment. Both of us prefer a system of free enterprise, and we shall both desire to lighten government controls as rapidly as the phenomenon of scarcity vanishes and conditions permit free enterprise to play its proper role. Both of us will find our industries still working largely on war orders, and the problems of conversion will be urgent. Both of us will want to make our contribution to the relief and reconstruction of the devastated countries, and we shall want to make that contribution in the way which will help the peoples of those regions get back to health and strength and to self-reliance as rapidly as possible. We shall both be interested in possible international arrangements about gold and currencies and international investment. And we shall both desire to increase the economic interchange between us and with others on the most fruitful basis possible.

On all these questions we can talk usefully together as we have agreed to do. Our discussions will become even more useful as we undertake to conduct them in an even larger framework, the framework of the whole United Nations. There is no disagreement anywhere as to what the United Nations want. They want full employment for their people at good wages and under good working conditions and the other physical and institutional arrangements that add up to freedom from want. But differences of opinion doubtless exist within and between the several countries as to the means to be adopted—divergencies may arise as to the desirability or efficacy of particular policies or measures.

An examination of the causes of any disagreement will usually reveal that it exists mainly because people are considering the question from different viewpoints, that the parties are basing their judgments on different or incomplete facts and different considerations. If both parties had the same facts and considerations in mind, and if each knew fully the reasons behind the position taken by the other, there would much more quickly be a meeting of minds.

This is true not only of individuals, but also of nations, and it suggests the need for joint as well as separate study of the facts and considerations relating to proposals aimed at attaining the desired ends. I believe that if the United Nations were to set up machinery for the purpose of assembling and studying all international aspects of problems under the general heading of freedom from want, and for assembling all the pertinent facts and considerations relating thereto, and for jointly analyzing all facts and considerations relating to measures or policies proposed for furthering the end in view, the controversies and conflicts of policy which have so long embittered relations in the international economic field, and therefore generally, might largely disappear. If the analysis were thorough enough and the problems of each country were fully understood by the others, solutions could be found that would serve the interests of all concerned. Nothing is more clear to my mind than this: if all aspects of an economic problem were explored, it would become apparent that the basic interests of all countries are largely common interests, that each country's economic problems are related to, and inseparable from, those of the others.

A United Nations study such as I have in mind would explore in a careful, thorough, and systematic way world problems in the economic field, toward the solution of which much progress must be made if we are to have anything approaching the goal of freedom from want in our own countries or elsewhere. People and governments here and everywhere are studying these problems, are searching for solutions. The plans of one government or group of governments may seem sound enough in the light of their own interests but may contain flaws which are visible from the viewpoint of other governments or countries. If the study to which I have referred did no more than detect and focus attention on such flaws, if it did no more than prevent the crystallization in one country or group of countries of ideas which are objectionable from the viewpoint of others, it would serve a highly useful purpose. It is, however, my hope and belief that a United Nations undertaking such as I have suggested would be able to formulate plans and recommendations of a constructive sort—to find, so to speak, common denominators which, in the net, would be advantageous to all. If we fail to begin such organized study and discussion now, there is danger that divergent views and policies may become crystallized, to the detriment of the common war effort and to the detriment of efforts to bring about a peace that will be more than a brief and uneasy interlude before another even more horrible and more destructive war devastates and depopulates the world.

My Government believes that the initiation of such studies is already overdue. If we do not make a start now, there is danger that we shall be brought together to make the peace with as many plans as there are governments. The day of complete victory cannot come too soon; we all give thanks to God for every advance we make toward that goal, at every sign of weakness in our enemies. Between now and that day we must endeavor to prepare ourselves to meet the responsibilities, and to make the most of the opportunities, that peace will bring.

I am glad to say that my Government intends at once to undertake discussions with other members of the United Nations as to the most practical and effective methods through which these vitally necessary conferences and consultations between us all can be held. It is my conviction that from these meetings a large measure of agreement will already be found to exist; that solutions will be available for such divergencies as may be apparent; and that in the last analysis it will be found that what may even appear to be fundamental obstacles can be resolved in the interest of the welfare of us all.

What the people of the United States are striving for, I am persuaded, is exactly what the people of Canada are striving for. They seek the attainment of the noble objectives set forth in the Atlantic Charter. They seek to achieve these ends, not because of any altruistic motives, not through the dictates of any theoretical idealism, but rather because they believe that the attainment of these objectives will be in their own self-interest— and I believe that in my own country we have learned through the bitter experience of the past quarter of a century that the most practical form of self-interest is enlightened self-interest.

We have seen beyond the shadow of any doubt that a policy of international cooperation which far too many told us twenty-four years ago was a policy of suicidal sentimentality was in fact a policy of advantageous hardheaded realism. Most of us have learned a great truth that is beginning to dawn upon the consciousness of many peoples in all parts of the globe, and that is that the real self-interest of one nation coincides with the permanent, with the ultimate, self-interests of other nations. For there is no people which will not benefit more by peace than by war. The preservation of peace and the practice of human tolerance must come to be recognized by every nation and by every government as the indispensable requisites of all peoples. Never again can humanity permit dictator demagogues once more to proclaim the alleged virile glories of war or the cruel falsehood that there exists a master race.

No rational man or woman today can question the

fact that had the nations of the world been able to create some effective form of international organization in
the years that followed the close of the last great world
war, and had they been able to bulwark that organization with judicial and police powers, the devastating
tragedy which humanity today is undergoing would
have been avoided. From the standpoint of material
self-interest alone, leaving aside every moral consideration, the lot of every one of our fellow citizens would
have been far better. No one can appraise the cost of
the present war in terms of life and human suffering.
But we can appraise its cost in material terms, and we
know that as a result of this material cost the standard
of living of every individual in every region of the world
will be impaired.

If at the conclusion of this war the governments of
the United Nations are not afforded by their peoples the
opportunity of collaborating together in effective policies of recovery, or of assuming a joint responsibility for
making completely sure that the peace of the world is
not again violated, there can be no result other than
utter disaster. The structure of our civilization is not so
tough as to make it conceivable that it would resist a
repetition of the present holocaust.

We have evolved here in the New World a system of
international relationships which constitutes perhaps
the highest achievement in the sphere of practical international living that civilized man has so far created.
From the historical standpoint it is very recent indeed,
but it has grown, gradually perhaps but nevertheless
steadily, throughout the period of the individual life of
the democracies of the Americas. It is a system in which

the smallest state is just as free to determine its own destiny as the largest state. It is a system where the smallest state feels just as secure as the largest state, because of its knowledge that its independence and integrity are a matter of vital concern to its more powerful neighbors, and because of its assurance that should its liberties be jeopardized by aggression coming from without the Western Hemisphere its more powerful neighbors will take the action necessary to repel that danger.

Every region of the world possesses its own peculiar problems, its own special advantages, and its own inherent difficulties. We hear much of the age-old rivalries which have persisted in Europe and in other quarters of the globe. But I think that we of the Americas can say that if twenty-two independent democracies such as those which occupy North, Central, and South America —of different races, of different languages, and of different origins—can achieve the measure of progress which we now have achieved towards a peaceful and humane relationship and towards profitable economic cooperation, that same form of relationship can be achieved in all regions of the world.

The creation of that same kind of decent international relationship by all peoples is the objective today of the United Nations. I am confident that after the unconditional surrender of our common enemies that objective will be attained. Through our continued cooperation the peace of the world can be maintained, for with the defeat and total disarmament of the Axis powers there can be no further conflict—if the United Nations stand together. We cannot permit this time that the supreme sacrifice which our sons and our brothers are making in the defense of our liberties shall be made in vain. Only through our combined efforts can we make certain that the victory which we will win in battle can become in fact the victory of peace.

Date Due			
JUL 14 '65			
APR 21 '86			